Experimental Study on Heat Transfer in Porous Media

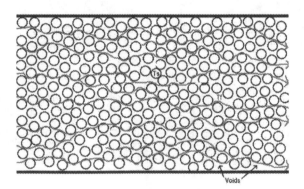

Experimental Study on Heat Transfer in Porous Media

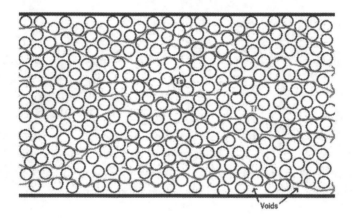

Dr. Beant Singh; Dr. Chanpreet Singh

PARTRIDGE
A Penguin Random House Company

To order additional copies of this book, contact
Partridge India
000 800 10062 62
orders.india@partridgepublishing.com

www.partridgepublishing.com/india

CONTENTS

DECLARATION

I hereby affirm that the work presented in this book is exclusively our own and there are no collaborators. It does not contain any work which is copied from any other source.

Dr Beant Singh
Principal, Punjab college of
Engg &Tech Lalru mandi
&
Dr Chanpreet Singh
Prof, Punabi University Patiala

PREFACE

The authors feel that reading of the book "EXPERIMENTAL STUDY ON HEAT TRANSFER IN POROUS MEDIA" will motivate the readers to organize their thoughts and improve in the field of porous media. The present work will be a valuable volume for the students undergoing research work and advanced study in this field. In order to give the knowledge of this field, one has normally refer to a number of latest research papers and text books related to the field. The results are evaluated after actual performing the experiments and compared with the standard results.

We are thankful to authors and publishers whose research work have been consulted freely for the preparation of this manuscript. Inspite of great care, errors might have crept in. It will be grateful to the teachers and candidates who point them out. The suggestions for improvement of this book will be thankfully accepted.

Beant Singh and Chanpreet Singh

CHAPTER 1

INTRODUCTION

1.1 GENERAL

In recent years considerable interest has been generated in the study of flow in porous media because of its natural occurrence and importance in both geophysical and engineering environments. The experimental study on heat transfer through the porous media finds wide applications in many fields like crude oil extractions, petroleum reservoirs, geothermal engineering, civil engineering, agricultural engineering, heat exchanges, coal combustors, solar collectors, electronic cooling, energy storage units, nuclear waste repositories and Biomedical engineering.

The porous media is heterogeneous system of solid and liquid in which the solid (like spherical beads) are closely packed and fluid passes through intervening space. The space between the matrixes is called voids or vovrens in which the fluid flows. These voids are normally interconnected and the path of fluid keeps changing from one void to another. Hence the flow through the voids provides intense mixing of the fluid with solid and spreading in longitudinal and transverse directions. During flow of fluid the acceleration forces are involved and relation between flow rate and pressure drop in the porous bed is not linear, hence the flow is considered as non Darcian flow. The thermal effect of porous medium is like a thermal sponge, absorbing energy in its solid phase when exposed to the hot fluid and releasing it to the cold fluid at a later stage of the cycle. As energy exchange takes place from and to the solid phase, temperature differentials are set up. The estimation of temperature differential between the two phases is important for the performance of the storage system. This is called thermal non-equilibrium. Energy and momentum equations can provide the required information for analyzing inter phase heat transfer in porous media. A lab scale experimental set up supported with software is also an efficient approach to measure the energy storage effects in porous media. The solid and fluid phase temperatures can be recorded with the variation of parameters such as flow rate, oscillating frequency and solid phase properties.

1.2 APPLICATIONS OF POROUS MEDIA

Heat transfer in porous media has many applications in various fields, heat sinks, cryogenic heat exchangers and absorption equipment. The important application fields are discussed in this section.

1.2.1 Environmental Application: The study of fluid flow in porous media has applications in many areas of geology and environmental science. The rock constitute the Earth's crust is a porous medium and deforms over geological timescales. The flow through, and erosion of, this medium by magma leads to such phenomena as layered magma chambers and volcanic eruptions. The flow of groundwater through soil and/or rock has important applications in agriculture and in pollution control. Other topics of interest include compaction of sedimentary basins and the phenomenon of frost heave, which occurs when groundwater freezes. As well as damaging roads and pavements, frost heave is responsible for geological formations like the stone garland.

1.2.2 Oil Recovery: One of the important applications of the porous media is extraction of oil from the porous rock and enhanced the oil recovery from the porous rock. The suction of viscous fluid from the porous medium is unstable, tending to leave behind the sizeable proportion of oil in small packets and increasing the extraction fraction is challenging factor. Sometimes the solvents are used to enhance the recovery. Another issue in the industry is up scaling from locally measured properties i.e. permeability. The useful preclusions can be made over much longer scale relevant to an oil well.

1.2.3 Medical Applications: The significant advances have achieved in applying porous media theory in modeling biomedical applications such as computational biology, tissue replacement production, drug delivery and advance medical imaging. Another important application of porous media includes diffusion process in the extracellular space, which is crucial for investigating central nerves system physiology. Also most of the tissues in the body (bone, cardiac, muscle) are deformable porous media. The proper functioning of such materials depends upon the flow of the blood, nutrients and so force through them. The porous medium models are used to understand different medical problems and their treatments at different conditions.

1.2.4 Heat Exchanger: Application of forced convection in porous media in the field of heat exchanger has gained extensive attention. The heat exchangers are a century old technology based on information's and concepts, used in large scale devices. The modern resolution of heat exchangers towards the cooling of electronic devices is a compact device with smaller dimensions. These low dimension devices operate at lower Reynolds number with structural porous media. In another study, the effect of radiation is taken into account and it is possible to describe the existence of an optimal parting density (porously) for minimum heat transfer across the porous media.

1.2.5 Regenerative Cry Coolers: The regenerator is a duct packed with some porous material. The porous material is selected such that it has sufficient thermal heat capacity, high heat transfer co-efficient and low flow friction. The designer of a cry cooler is mainly concerned with achieving specifically net refrigeration at that temperature with minimum input. Regenerative cry coolers are used in variety of application like pulse tube cry coolers and sterling coolers. These devices are typically used in applications which demand small net refrigeration at temperature below 100^0 k. Applications which require these types of refrigeration and super conducting electronic, magnetic resonance image are infrared focal plane arrays. Other applications include gas huge fraction of nitrogen, magneto cardiograph using super conducting quantum interference devices and military weapons systems.

In addition to the above applications the porous media is applied to many aspects of agricultural and engineering because mass, momentum and energy transport in porous media are closely associated with various physical phenomenon and practical problem such as thermal insulation of building, heat pipe system coupled with heat pipe source, cooling of electronic equipment, cooling of turbine blades etc.

1.3 PRESENT WORK

In the present research work small scale lab experiments are performed on porous media and convective heat transfer between the solid and liquid phase is analyzed at different flow rate. The energy storage equations are used to find the amount of heat stored by porous media and the heat retrieved by the fluid used. The experiments are performed at different flow rate and by varying the inlet hot water temperature. The response of porous bed is analyzed by considering the frequency response of porous bed, front amplitude, front speed and front spread. The thermal equilibrium is calculated to study the heat storage effects.

The experimental set up is designed in such a way that the flow is oscillatory in which the fluid is entering at both of the domain ends periodically. The accuracy and reliability of measuring instruments are checked for standard results. The experimental set up consists of porous bed in which spherical solid beads are closely packed and water flows around the beads. The diameter of the bead is less than 1/10 the diameter of bed to maintain the flat flow. The direction of flow is controlled by valves fitted on each end of the bed. Flow rate is measured by adjustable rotameter and value of flow can be adjusted at any particular value. The temperature of the bed is sensed by K- type thermocouples inserted in the bed. It generates 10 mille Volts per degree Celsius rise of the temperature. The thermocouples are inserted at equal distance apart leaving required length at both ends to minimize the end effects. The bed has effective length of 660 mm for energy storage and energy retrieval. Thermocouple cold junction compensation circuit is fabricated to make the reference temperature as zero degrees Celsius. The circuit has flexibility of calibration with simple a multi meter. The analog signal obtained from thermocouple is converted into digital form with the help 2213 ADD LINK DAQ card. It is 16 channel high sensitive card which generate 50 digital output in 10 seconds. With the help of 8.2 version lab view software the observations are recorded in the PC. The repeatability of the apparatus was checked for three different type of bed and found satisfactory. The flow of fluid is considered as turbulent flow as rate of flow is high (Re on the basis of radius is above 150). Single fluid saturated flow is maintained in the bed and air bubbles if any is removed in warm up period. The flow of fluid in porous material is complex and velocity pressure relation is not linear. The flow is considered as non Darcian flow. The fluid path is tortuous due to presence of solid material. The flow of fluid in porous media is shown in Figure 1.1 in which the lines show the flow of fluid.

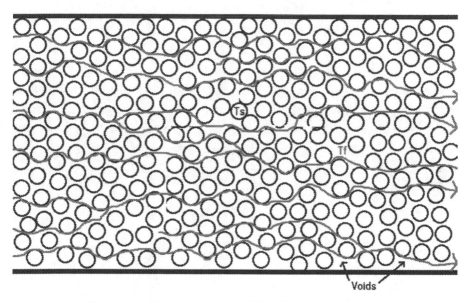

Figure 1.1: Tortuous path of fluid in porous media

It provides intense mixing of solid and liquid. The hot and cold water is flowing through porous bed alternately in opposite direction. The temperature fluctuates between the maximum and the minimum value. The front amplitude and phase lag is analyzed at different flow rate. The front speed and front spread are measured and presented graphically. The cyclic temperatures in sine wave form are obtained. As the heat energy is stored by the solid media, there exists a temperature difference between the solid and the liquid phases of the porous media, which is called thermal non-equilibrium. The thermal non-equilibrium plays an important role in energy storage system. Thermal non equilibrium between solid and fluid is presented graphically. The amount of heat stored and retrieved is calculated for each cycle with the help of energy equations. As the different material have different thermal properties, the two different materials (Steel and Glass) used as their thermal properties are distinct. The amount of heat stored and retrieved is observed at different flow rate by the spherical shape porous media of different materials of different diameters. Experiments are carried out on two different sizes of steel spheres and corresponding size of glass spheres. Amount of heat transfer in oscillating flow is calculated by using the energy equations. The value of the energy storage and retrieval is represented for different flow rate, size and materials. The heat exchange values are also compared. In all the experiments the saturated & single phase flow at a constant head is maintained.

The effect of the change in particle at different flow rate is studied. The present study is to study the inter phase heat transfer in porous media while using the oscillating flow with the different particle size of the solid phase and to study the effects of flow rate on thermal parameters of the bed with the different input temperature at constant head and saturated flow.

CHAPTER 2

LITERATURE SURVEY
AND PROBLEM FORMULATION

2.1 INTRODUCTION

The application of heat transfer in porous medium has gained importance in the last few years and scientists have carried out many researches in this particular field with significant results. The porous media contains a large number fluid particles flowing in pores, it is very difficult to determine their initial and final position. By considering the macroscopic level over a representative volume, the fluid flow problems are solved and the flow is considered as saturated flow. The literature survey for the porous media invarious fields like flow, oscillatory flow, thermal non equilibrium and heat transfer is carried out.

Nield & Bejan has established the relations of various parameters involved in porous media. The convection in porous media was explained with the help of research papers. The terms seepage velocity, porosity, permeability, and momentum equation and Brickman's equation are explained as these are important for studying the flow in porous media. Heat transfer and mass transfer in porous media with the various effects like local thermal equilibrium, chemical reaction effects pressure change etc are explained. The text book gives the basic idea about the flow in porous media and heat transfer at various parameters.

M.Kaviany: The principles of heat transfer in porous media text book made an attempt to integrate transport, reaction and phase change in porous media. It explains the heat transfer influenced and brooded coverage of phase change. The high frequency flow and inlet temperature oscillating fluid phase used for storage and release of heat is explained.

2.2 FLOWS IN POROUS MEDIA

The porous media consists of a solid matrix with the interconnected voids and fluid passes through these voids. The two types of flow occurs in porous media namely saturated and unsaturated. The flow in which the voids are completely filled with fluid is saturated fluid. In the pore scale, parameters like velocity and pressure will be clearly irregular and difficult to measure. In the typical experiments volume averaged quantities are measured as volume. Space-averaged (microscopic) quantizes change in a regular manner with respect to space and time, and hence are amenable to theoretical analysis.

Ramananthan [2010] has reviewed the existing work on pressure drop calculations in two phase flow through porous media. The experiments are carried out by taking two immiscible liquids and calculated the capillary pressure and macroscopic velocity. Then the gas-liquid flow through the porous bed is analyzed. By taking the limitation of Darcy's law, the individual single phase pressure drops are estimated by the Ergun's law. It is analyzed that how the pressure changes over the different regimes and the analysis is carried out in two phase thermal flow.

Giovanni Climatti [2009] presented the method of reducing the PDE system of the flow of viscous fluid in a porous medium to simple problem for laplacian. It is discussed that in previous papers, the onset of natural convection, non linear stability, existence and uniqueness of solution were thoroughly examined and boundary conditions were set on velocity of the flow. By considering the different approach, the pressure is assumed as datum on the boundary and the seepage velocity v is induced. As per Darcy Law the seepage velocity is given by

$$v = -\frac{k}{\mu}\nabla p \qquad (2.1)$$

Where k is the permeability, μ is dynamic viscosity and p is pressure. The velocity and thermal conductivity are allowed to depend on the temperature. The nearly explicit computation and uniqueness solutions are obtained.

Alabi *et.al* [2009] has investigated that the saturated flow obeys the Darcy law when the flow is laminar flow. The flow deviates from the Darcy's law whenever there is variation in the porosity and hydraulic gradient. By considering the effect of the porosity of any porous medium and at any hydraulic gradient, a general equation for both laminar and turbulent flow is proposed with boundary considerations. It has been investigated that as per Darcy law at lower porosity volume flux (q) relates with hydraulic (i) as

$$q = ci \qquad\qquad (2.2)$$

Where c is an empirical constant.

Amaniford *et al.* [2007] has investigated the effects of electrical double layer (EDL) near the solid liquid interface, on three dimension heat transfer characteristic and pressure drop of water flow through a rectangular micro channel. EDL will originate the additional force for the modifications of Navier-stokes and energy equations. These equations were solved numerically by considering the flow as laminar flow over a controlled volume. It is analyzed that EDL at high electrical potential affects the flow significantly and deviates from flow characteristic described in classical fluid mechanics.

Namgyem Jeong *et al.* [2006] studied the micro flow through three dimensional granular and fibrous porous media at different Knudsen number by using lattice Boltzmann's method. The granular materials of rounded inclusions results as per existing empirical and numerical co-relations between the permeability and Reynolds number, but sharp corner inclusions results do not agree with the existing empirical and numerical co-relations. Then the new co-relation for the Darcy-Forcheimer drag for different shapes and arrangement is proposed. The results for fibrous materials were agreed with the existing numerical relations. Further the new correlation between the permeability, the porosity and Knudsen number for the both granular and fibrous porous media is proposed.

Seo Young [1994] made a numerical study of heat transfer characteristics from forced pulsating flow in a channel filled with fluid saturated porous media. By considering the uniform channel wall temperature, the Brinkman-Forchhinmer extended equation is used. The two dimensional equation were solved with finite elements techniques. It is analyzed that in comparison with non pulsating flow, the pulsating flow brings reduction of heat transfer in existence region where as heat transfer is mediate in downstream regions. Influence of heat capacity ratio, thermal conductivity ratio and Darcy No on the flow of heat transfer characteristics is scrutinized.

2.2.1 Summary for Fluid Flow in Porous Media

Year	Author Name	Subject
2010	Ramananthan	Reviewed the existing work on pressure drop calculations in two phase flow through porous media. By taking two immiscible liquids and calculated the capillary pressure and macroscopic velocity
2009	Giovanni Climatti	The method of reducing the PDE system for the flow of viscous fluid in a porous medium
2009	Alabi *et.al*	The saturated flow obeys the Darcy law when the flow is laminar flow. The flow deviates from the Darcy's law whenever there is variation in the porosity and hydraulic gradient
2007	Amaniford *et al.*	Effects of electrical double layer (EDL) near the solid liquid interface, on three dimension heat transfer characteristic and pressure drop of water flow through a rectangular micro channel
2006	Namgyem Jeong *et al.*	Studied the micro flow through two dimensional and three dimensional granular and fibrous porous media at different Knudsen number by using lattice Boltsann method

1994	Seo Young *et al.*	A numerical study of heat transfer characteristics from forced pulsating flow in a channel filled with fluid saturated porous media

2.3 OSCILLATING FLOW IN POROUS MEDIA

Heat transfer in porous media can be enhanced by increasing surface area in contact with the fluid. The physics of fluid flow in porous media filled with metal particles or spheres is investigated widely. In the oscillating flow hot and cold fluid flows through the porous bed alternately for equal interval of time. The oscillating flow shows the different results as compared to plan flow.

Mehmet *et al.* [2012] studied the heat transfer in porous media under oscillating flow experimentally. Number of experiments was carried out with different frequencies, flow displacement length and heat input for steel balls. It is observed that the local Nussuelt number based upon the time averaged wall and bulk temperature increases with frequency and maximum fluid displacement. The space cycle averaged Nussuelt number increases with kinetic Reynolds number and non-dimensional fluids displacement.

Trefry *et al.* [2010] explained that the Geo fluid may experience pressure and temperature effects in porous media which are periodic in nature and drive the momentum equation beyond the normal Darcy regime. In this paper the special inversion of a generalized geo fluid momentum equation in the context of time periodic boundary condition is described. It is shown that the generalized momentum equation results in frequency domain responses which are governed by second order equation.

J.C.Umavathi *et al.* [2009] has discussed the unsteady flow and heat transfer is a horizontal composite porous medium. The two parallel permeable plates are considered with half of distance between them filled by a fluid saturate porous layer and other by clear viscous fluid. A closed form of the solutions is analytical and oscillation amplitude is less than one. The non periodic and periodic values were determined at varies parametric condition. The values of velocity and temperature are described by the different graphs. By considering the viscous and Darcian dispersion terms in energy equation, the Partial differential equation for flow and heat transfer is solved. The velocity and temperature decreases as viscosity ratio increases and increase with the increase in oscillation amplitude. The effect of the Prandtl number and Eckert numbers decrease the thermal state of the channel.

Bouvier et al. [2005] have analyzed experimentally and theoretically the heat transfer parameters in an oscillating fluid in a pipe. A specially designed instrumentation test rig measure the temperature in the fluid at various locations from the heated wall, solid fluid interface temperature and instances heat flow near the wall measured in an oscillating flow, subjected to the wall heating. A comparison with analytical result is good.

Fu *et al.* [2001] analyzed experimentally the heat transfer in porous channel subjected to oscillating flow. A heated porous section is subjected to oscillatory airflow at inlet bulk temperature. The experimental results show that the surface temperature distribution for oscillating flow is more uniform than that for steady flow. A porous media subjected to oscillatory flow can act a good heat sink. A porous media in presence of oscillatory flow is considered as an effective method of rapid heat dissipation. A porous media has a layer effective solid surface area that can store and retrieve energy during oscillatory flow.

2.3.1 Summary for oscillating flow

Year	Author Name	Subject
2012	Mehmet *et al.*	Studied the heat transfer in porous media under oscillating flow.
2010	Trefry *et al.*	Geo fluid may experience pressure and temperature effect in porous media which are periodic in nature and drive the momentum equation.
2009	J.C.Umavathi *et al.*	Discussed the unsteady flow and heat transfer is a horizontal composite porous medium.
2005	Bouvier *et al.*	Analyzed experimentally and theoretically the heat transfer parameters in an oscillating fluid in a pipe.

| 2001 | Fu *et al.* | Analyzed experimentally the heat transfer in porous channel subjected to oscillating flow. |

2.4 INTER PHASE HEAT TRANSFER

The porous structures are utilized extensively in modern technical and engineering applications. Porous construction material with regular structure is used for cooling of thermally intense components of advanced technical equipments, in particularly for cooling blades of the high temperature gas turbines. Due to wide application of porous media in the different field, it is essential to find out the heat transfer between solid and liquid phase.

Gazy *et al.* [2012] had numerical analysis on the effect of particle diameter of packed bed of spherical sizes. The analysis was based on two phase energy thermal non equilibrium model. The investigation were carried out on cylinder to particle diameter ratio from 10-100 at wide range of flow rate. It is observed the presence of porous materials around the cylinder increases over all heat transfer and increases pressure drop in the bed. The large particle diameter increases the heat transfer and decreases pressure drop.

Mukhopadhyay & Layek [2009] presented the heat transfer analysis for the boundary layer for corrective flow of an in compressible fluid past a plate embedded in porous media. By taking the radiation effect the numerical solutions are obtained for steady forced corrective boundary layer flow. It is observed that the effect of permeability of medium on various incompressible fluids is to increase the fluid velocity by reducing the drag on flow. As the suction skin friction increases the rate of heat transfer increases and thermal radiation temperature decreases. The combined effect of suction and thermal radiation can be used as means of cooling and rate of heat transfer increases with increasing Prandtl number.

Das *et al.* [2009] has discussed the effect of mass transformation for free convective flow and heat transfer of a viscous incompressible electrically conducting fluid past a vertical porous plate through porous medium. The effects of the important flow parameters such as magnetic parameters, permeability parameter, Grashof number for heat transfer, heat source parameter and rarefaction parameter on the velocity of the flow field are analyzed. The flow in the medium is due to Buoyancy force covered by the temperature difference between wall and medium is assumed in equation. The governing equations of the flow field are solved analytically and the expressions for velocity, temperature, skin friction and the heat flux in terms of Nusselt number are obtained.

It is observed that the velocity of flow varies vastly with the variation of flow parameters such as magnetic parameter, crashed number of heat & mass transfer, heat source parameter & Prandtl number. The effect of magnetic parameter on the velocity of flow keeping other parameters is shown graphically. It is observed that the amplitude of heat transfer and rate of heat transfer are least for the Mercury and highest for the water.

Mahamed [2009] presented the effect of first order homogenous chemical reaction, thermal radiation, heat source and thermal diffusion on unsteady magneto hydro dynamics (MHD) double diffusion from convection fluid flow past a vertical porous plate. It is assured that the plate is embedded in porous media and moves with constant velocity in the flow direction and in the presence of transverse magnetic field. By taking the viscous and Darcy resistance into account the MHD term is desired formulae the Navier stoke equation. From the cartelism framed reference equations are reduced to partial differential equation in the ordinary equation of dimensional less form. The numerical calculations for the distribution of velocity, temperature concentration across boundary layer are carried out. It is observed that for different value of radiation parameter the velocity increases with boundary generated the binary force increases which increase the flow rate. The velocity profile for different value of Grashof no (Gr) is described.

Polykor *et al.* [2009] has investigated the heat transfer in envelope porous network material under laboratory conditions. The experiments were carried with wide range of Reynolds number at minimum possible flow rates. The numerical experiments were carried out for the additional data by varying the thermo physical properties at geometrical and physical parameters. The result of joint laboratory and numerical experiments, the data on heat transfer is obtained. The equations of motion and energy are used for calculating air flow, temperature in the air and in the solid frame of porous wall.

Morcelo [2009] in his paper on the laminar heat transfer in a porous channel is numerical simulator with two energy equations for conduction and convection. The macroscopic equations for conductivity, momentum and energy transport for the fluid and solid phases were presented. The numerical methodology is based upon control volume approach with a boundary fitted non orthogonal co-ordinate system. Fully developed forced convection in a porous channel bounded by parallel plate is considered. Solutions for Nusselt number along the channel are presented for laminar flows. Result simulates the effect of Reynolds's number, porosity, particle size and solid to fluid thermal conductivity ratio on Nusselt number, which is defined on both solid and fluid phases.

Akdag *et al.* [2009] have predicted the heat transfer from a surface having constant heat flux subjected to oscillating annular flow by using artificial neural networks (ANN). There artificial neural network consisting of very simple and highly interconnected processors collect neural is a computational structure inspired by biological neural system. The investigation is carried out by a special apparatus to estimate the heat transfer characteristics as a function of some input parameters namely frequency amplitude, heat flux and filling heights. Result of the experiments and ANN are in close agreement with error less than 5%. The study showed that ANN could be used effectively for modeling oscillating flow heat transfer in a vertical annular duct.

Shadi Mahjoob and Kambiz [2008] has discussed about the metal foam heat exchanger. As the metal foams are a class of porous material with low densities and novel thermal properties. The metal foam heat exchangers have advantages over other available commercial heat exchangers due to more heat transfer surface area and large boundary layer disruption. The pressure drop and heat transfer co-relations for three types of metal foam heat exchangers were analyzed. In the first type the co-relation are independent of heat exchanger geometry and function of microstructure of foam. The pressure drop can be estimated by Ergun Equation. In the second type the co-relations are developed for foam filled tube heat exchanger. Based on these co-relations the foam heat exchanger can be designed for application where inner tube and outer tubes are filled with foam metals. The third type relates to the metal foam channel heat exchangers filled with foam metals. The local thermal non equilibrium form of energy equations is applied. It was investigated that the foam heat exchangers have considerable better performance.

Rahman & Sultana [2008] has explained the heating effects on boundary layer of micro polar over the porous plate with variable heat flux in the presence of radiation. As micro polar fluid is the fluid with internal structure in which coupling between spin of each particle and the macroscopic velocity field is considered. By using the Darcy- Forcheimer model momentum micro-rotation and energy equations are numerical solved. The variation of non-dimensional velocity, micro-ration and energy equations is studied. The effects of various parameters were examined and it is observed that the skin friction co-efficient increases with increase of suction parameter, coupling parameters, none zero micro rotation parameter and spin gradient viscosity. Also the rate of heat transfer increases with increase of suction parameters, buoyancy parameter, coupling parameter and non-zero micro rotation, while radiation has decreasing effect on velocity & temperature.

Frey *et al.* [2007] has presented a mathematical model based on heat transfer in a flow through a porous media based on the continuum theory of mixtures. A mechanical modeling for a non-classical approach for the heat transfer in a flow through a porous channel has been presented. This model, which is based on the continuum theory of mixtures, generates a hydrodynamic problem analogous to the steady-state Stokes problem, except for the momentum source term – which is used as input for the thermal problem. The boundary value problem consisting of two coupled partial equations, one describing the fluid constituent energy balance and the other the solid one. (The coupling term is an energy source term.) A PetrovGalerkin formulation has been employed to approximate the equations describing the non-isothermal advective flow. For low Péclet regime, the results have pointed out thermal equilibrium between both constituents. For high and very high Pécletflows, stabilization strategies proved to be essential, being able to capture accurately smooth thermal boundary-layers near the channel walls and, for very high Péclet flows, the PetrovGalerkin formulation simulated a quasi-hyperbolic exact solution. A Petrov Galerkin formulation is employed to approximate the equations described by the non isothermal adjective flow. It is observed that at very high Peclet flow, stabilization strategies to be essential and able to capture accurately smooth thermal boundary layer near the channel well. The petrov-Galerkm simulated the grassy hyperbolic exact solutions.

Byun *et al.* [2006] analyzed the thermal behavior of porous medium under the oscillating flow. By considering the two dimensional equation, the two parameters were identified as ratio of thermal capacities between solid and fluid phase and ratio of interstitial heat conductance between the phases to fluid thermal capacity. With the variation of solid and fluid temperature the analytical solution were obtained. The local thermal equilibrium is suggested a simple form the ratio of two time scales intrinsically involved in any heat transfer in porous media.

In the recent yearly the porous medium with saturated binary fluid has gained attention due to its relevance in many natural & industrial problems like migration of moisture contained in fibrous maculation, grain storage, the transport of contaminants in saturated soils etc. Earlier the Nield (1967) has predicated on double diffusive natural convection in porous media with the case of a horizontal layer heated and salted from the bottom.

The Soret induced correction is a horizontal porous media subjected to cross heat flux is analyzed. The mathematical model for the system is derived. The governing equation h is derived in terms of stream function, temperature and concentration.

Leong and Jin [2005] has carried out the experimental on heat transfer of oscillating flow through a channel filled with aluminum foam subjected to constant wall heat flux. The experiment measurement of surface temperature distribution on the walls, velocity of flows and pressure drops across the test section were carried out. The characteristics of pressure drops, the effect of dimensionless amplitude of displacement and dimensionless frequency of oscillating flow on heat transfer in porous channel were analyzed. It was observed that the heat transfer in oscillating flow is significantly increased by imploring porous media in plate channel. The Nusselt Number is effective increased by increasing the Reynolds's number and dimensionless amplitude of flow displacement data, a co-relation equation of the Nusselt number with dimensionless parameter Pew and A_o is obtained for porous channels.

You Ming Chen [2005] have investigated the heat and mass transfer characteristics of combined vertical films type observed evaporate heat exchanger. An experiment was carried out and parameter like flow rate of inlet prime solution and water, inlet brine concentration and pressure difference in the absorbed are analyzed. The methods of analogy between heat and mass transfer near the film surface are used to calculate the interfacial temperature and concentration of brine function based upon the experimental cut. The co-relation of mass transfer co-efficient has been derived. The overall heat transfer co-efficient practically remains constant compared to inlet brine Reynolds number considering the different characteristics of heat transfer between film surface region and wall region a model has been proposed and successfully applied to evaluate the heat transfer co-efficient.

Jan-Shery *et al.* [2000] has evaluated the heat and mass enhancement of liquid film evaporation by covering porous layer on the plate. A two dimensional steady laminar boundary layer model is adapted for gas and liquid streams. The non-Dorcian effect and boundary effects are considered saturated porous media. The effect of porous layer heat and mass transfer is evaluated. The property like Reynolds of porous layer on performance of liquid film evaporation is examined. It is concluded that for lower porosity and layer thickness will produce higher interfacial temperature and mass concentrations. The application value of layer thickness is 0.001- 0.005 for practical application. The lower value of relative humidity leads to higher Nussult No. and Sherwood Number. As the Lewis number increases, larger heat transfer rate and mass flow rate are achieved.

Sumrerng Jugjui and Chanen Chuenchit [2000] have given the observation for the conversion of energy from the low grade fuel and producing thermal energy. It is predicted that cyclic flow reversal combination (CFRC) in porous medium is a promising approach for further application. The CFRC is advantageous from the aspect of fuel conservation, efficiency, and combustion intensity and emission pollutants, because of its ability for creating internal heat recirculation from hot exhaust gases to unburned mixtures as compared to convention burns. From the porous combustor heat exchange (PCHE) quipped with CFRC was developed for abstracting heat flow low grade gases fuel. The experiment is arranged in such a way that inner cylinder is porous combustor which works as radiant burner equipment with CFRC. The outer cylinder is porous heat exchange act as integral function of radioactive heat absorbed. The radioactive heat flux converted from the heat of combustion is converted into substantial increase in enthalpy.

Morthy and P singh [1999] analyzed the Forchheimer fluid convection heat and mass transfer near the vertical surface embedded in fluid saturated porous media. The heat transfer in case of saturated porous media is studied with relation to different application like dynamic of hot underground springs, heat exchange between soil and atmosphere flow of moisture through porous industrial material, heat exchanged with fluidized beds etc. The mass transfer in isothermal conditions has been studied with application of mixing of fresh and salt water in aquifers, spreading of solid in fluidized beds and crystal washes, salt leaching in soils etc. The objective this study is to analysis the effect of lateral mass flux on the free convection heat and mass transfer from a vertical wall in a fluid saturated porous medium with Forchheimer flow model. The differential equation with boundary conditions is solved and heat & mass transfer co-efficient were determined in terms of Nusselt and Sherwood number.

The graphs were platted for Nusselt and Sherwood number against buoyancy ratio (N), Lewis No. (Le) and mass flux (fw). It is shown that Nusselt and Sherwood number increases as the value of buoyancy ratio increases.

2.4.1 Summary of Inter phase Heat Transfer

Year	Author Name	Subject
2012	Gazy *et al.*	Numerical analysis on the effect of particle diameter of packed bed of spherical sizes
2009	Mukhopadhyay & Layek	Heat transfer analysis for the boundary layer for corrective flow of an in compressible fluid past a plate embedded in porous media
2009	Das *et al.*	Effect of mass transformation for corrective flow and heat transfer of a viscous incompressible electrically conducting fluid pool a verbal porous plate through porous medium

2009	Mahamed	Effect of first order homogenous chemical reaction, thermal radiation, heat source and thermal diffusion on unsteady MHD double diffusion from convection fluid flow past a vertical porous plate.
2009	Polykor *et al*	Heat transfer in envelope porous network material under laboratory conditions
2009	Morcelo	Laminar heat transfer in a porous channel is numerical simulator with two energy equations for conduction and convection
2009	Akdag	Heat transfer from a surface having constant heat flux subjected to oscillating annular flow by using artificial neural networks
2008	Shadi mahjoob and Kambiz	About the metal foam heat exchanger
2008	Rahman & Sultana	Heating effects on boundary layer of micro polar over the porous plate with variable heat flux in the presence of radiation
2007	Frey *et al.*	A mathematic model based on heat transfer in a flow through a porous media based on the continuum theory of mixtures
2006	Byun *et al.*	Thermal behavior of porous medium under the oscillating flow
2005	Leong and Jin	Experiment on heat transfer of oscillating flow through a channel filled with aluminum foam subjected to constant wall heat flux
2000	Jan-Shery *et al.*	Evaluated the heat and mass enhancement of liquid film evaporation by covering porous layer on the plate
2000	Sumrerng Jugjui and Chanen Chuenchit	Energy conversion from the low grade fuel for producing the thermal energy and suggested that cyclic flow reversal combination (CFRC) in porous medium
1999	Morthy and P singh	Forchheimer fluid convection heat and mass transfer near the vertical surface embedded in fluid saturated porous media

2.5 THERMAL NON EQUILIBRIUM

There is increasing interest in convection in local thermal non-equilibrium (LTNE) porous media. This is where the solid skeleton and the fluid may have different temperatures. There is also increasing interest in thermal wave motion, especially at the micro scale and nano scale, and particularly in solids. The thermal non equilibrium in a fluid-saturated non Darcy porous medium is allowing the solid and fluid parts to be at different temperatures. Thermal non equilibrium is key for heat transfer between liquid and solid.

Kambiz [2013] in this paper discussed few concepts related to thermal non equilibrium and about the heat flux bifurcation in porous media. The temperature distribution in solid and liquid phases was explained for saturated channel subjected to constant wall heat flux boundary conditions. The attempt is made to study the heat flux bifurcation phenomenon in porous medium under local thermal non equilibrium conditions. The exact solutions for both the solid and fluid temperature distribution for convective heat transfer within a channel fully filled with porous medium subjected to constant wall heat flux boundary conditions with internal heat generation in both fluid & solid phases are obtained.

Nield [2012] analyze the thermal boundary conditions at the interface between porous media and fluid when there is local thermal non equilibrium at five sets of boundary conditions and analytical solutions for fluid temperature and solid temperature are obtained. The details of thermal boundary conditions at the interface between fluids are studied. It is observed that temperature distribution during local thermal non equilibrium in solid phase is different from the distribution in fluid phase. By describing the problem alternate interpretation for the solution is presented.

Kyhani *et al.* [2011] examine the effects of temperature due to sudden change in boundary conditions and large heat transfer in the porous media. Two energy equations in transient state and in the presence of heat generating state are used in each phase. Compact finite difference method for calculations of derivatives is used. The value of heat transfer in the initial and final stage was studied. The result shows that effect of heat generating and local thermal non equilibrium is restrained for very late times and graph slope decreases to zero. Also, effect of different non dimensional parameters on behavior of temperature gradients is verified. When diffusivity ratio increases, time to counteract heat generation effect increases. Fluid and solid graphs are stabilized in the negative value of temperature gradient with the constant slop zero and different diffusivity ratio do not affect on this value.

Chanpreet *et al.* [2009] studied the energy storage in fluid saturated porous media subjected to oscillatory flow and the transient thermal effect in a porous medium subjected to oscillatory flow of hot and cold fluids are discussed. The governing equations of thermal non equilibrium model have been numerically solved any finite difference scheme. The amplitude of temperature fluctuation, a parameter relating to energy storage is seen to vary significantly with distant and time. The storage of energy is largely governed by fluid to solid phase thermal storage capacity ratio. Effects arising from the change in bed parameters are discussed.

Roy *et al.* [2006] define the empirical parameter for an initial thermal non equilibrium porous media model for use in computational fluid dynamics (CFD) codes for simulation of sterling regenerators. Sterling ID regenerative models used in sterling engine design uses thermo non equilibrium model. It is observed that regenerator matrix and gas average temperature can differ by several degree at given initial axial location and time during the cycle by using a NASA regeneration research grant, the parameter in non-equilibrium porous media like hydrodynamics dispersion perm easily, inertia co-efficient fluid effective thermal conductivity, solid heat transfer co-efficient are calculated. It is suggested that the thermal non equilibrium model incorporated with CFD codes with improves the ability over the thermal equilibrium model.

B. Stroughan [2006] has demonstrated the equivalence between nonlinear stability and linear instability model for local thermal non equilibrium convection in a Darcy porous medium when the layer is undergoing a constant angular rotation abut on axis in the same direction as gravity. It is shown that nonlinear stability threshold for convection with thermal non equilibrium model is exactly same as linear instability boundary. These results are suitable for porous medium equations of Darcy, Forchheimer and Brinkman. This optimal result is important because it shows that the linear zed instability theory has captured the physics of the onset of convection.

Muralidhar and Suzuki [2001] have analyzed for the pulsating flow of gas and the accompanying heat transfer within a regenerator made from mesh screens. A flow model is developed taking the mesh as a non-Darcy, thermally non-equilibrium porous medium. A harmonic analysis technique is used for solving the fully developed but unsteady gas flow in the regenerator. Based on the flow solution thus obtained, slowly evolving symmetric unsteady thermal fields are solved numerically over a wide range of frequencies by making use of the finite volume method. Presentation is made of the friction factor and regenerator effectiveness. Effects of Reynolds number and frequency on the temperature profile and the transient behavior of the system are discussed. The importance of a thermal time constant of the system and length-to-radius ratio of the regenerator demonstrated. An oscillatory flow of gas was used with metallic mesh screens over a wide range of Reynolds number, domain lengths and frequencies quantities such as the function factor and regenerative effectiveness have been calculated.

2.5.1 Summary of Thermal Non Equilibrium

Year	Author Name	Subject
2013	Kambiz Vafai &Kun Yang	A note on Local Thermal Non-equilibrium in Porous Media and Heat Flux Bifurcation in porous media.
2012	A. Nield	Analyze the thermal boundary conditions at the interface between porous media and fluid when there is local thermal non equilibrium
2011	Kyhani *et al.*	Effects of temperature due to sudden change in boundary conditions and large heat transfer in the porous media.
2009	Chanpreet *et al.*	Energy storage in fluid saturated porous media subjected to oscillatory flow and the transient thermal effect in a porous medium subjected to oscillatory flow

2006	Roy *et al.*	Empirical parameter for an initial thermal non equilibrium porous media model for use in computational fluid dynamics (CFD) codes for simulation of sterling regenerators
2006	B. Straughan	Equivalence between nonlinear stability and linear instability bounds for local thermal non equilibrium convection in a darcy porous medium
2001	Muralidhar and Suzuki	Oscillatory flow and heat transfer in regenerators using the thermal no-equilibrium model

2.6 CLOSURE

In the review of flow in porous media, the pressure drop in two phase flow is presented and the methods of reducing the partial differential equation for viscous fluid are described. The limitation of saturated flow for Darcy law and deviation with porosity is discussed. The numerical study of heat transfer characteristics from forward pulsating flow in channel is described. In the heat transfer in the oscillating flow the variation of pressure and temperature of the geofluid flow in porous media is described. Attention is made to describe the unsteady flow and heat transfer in porous media. Numerical analysis on the effect of particle diameter in packed bed is shown. The heat transfer analysis for the boundary layer for corrective flow of incompressible fluid is presented. Numerical simulation of laminar heat transfer in porous channel for equation 2 is discussed. A mathematical model of heat transfer through a porous media based on continuum theory of mixture is presented. Heat transfer from the surface having constant heat flux is subjected to oscillating flow is discussed. The convection heat and mass transfer near the vertical surface embedded in a fluid saturated porous media is described. The thermal equilibrium plays a key role in the energy transfer; the attention is given to present the interface between solid and liquid in local thermal non-equilibrium. The amount of energy storage in oscillating flow and thermal effect is presented. Heat transfer and oscillating flow in regenerators using non-equilibrium modes is described. Present study is to experimentally study the interface heat transfer between solid and liquid in the oscillating flow, also to find out the affect of different material and size of porous media at different flow rates.

CHAPTER 3

MATHEMATICAL MODELS
FOR FLOW AND HEAT TRANSFER
IN POROUS MEDIA

3.1 INTRODUCTION

A porous medium is a medium that is partially occupied with solid material, which is interconnected. The portion of space that is not occupied by the solid material is also mostly interconnected. The solid material is normally called the solid matrix and the nonsolid portion is called pores or voids. Owing to the very complex and unknown nature of the geometry of a porous medium, the analysis of transport phenomena in porous media is difficult. It is for this reason that some averaging procedures have to be adopted

In the flow of fluid analysis and heat transfer. It is necessary to find out the parameter, which affects the exchange of heat from liquid to solid phase and vice versa. Whenever there is difference of temperature between the solid phase and the liquid phase the thermal non equilibrium exists between the solid and the liquid phases. The thermal non equilibrium between the fluid and solid phase is the key to energy exchange between the two phases.

3.2 FLUID FLOW EQUATION

The porous media consist of spherical balls and fluid flows through the interconnected pores. When a single fluid fills the pores of the porous medium, it is said to be saturated. For flow of a single fluid through a fixed solid matrix, a commonly used mathematical model is:

$$v = -\frac{k}{\mu}\nabla p \tag{3.1}$$

Darcy [1856] originally discovered it. This equation has found utility in a wide range of applications and is a popular starting point in the analysis of various problems. Here v is the Darcy velocity, different from the true fluid velocity prevailing in the pores. It is an average velocity at a point surrounded by porous region. Further, p is the fluid pressure, μ is the dynamic viscosity and K is the permeability of the porous medium. Darcy Law is valid as long as Reynolds number based on particle diameter is between 0 and 10, such that the viscous effects are dominant.

3.3 REPRESENTATIVE ELEMENTARY VOLUME

The path through the pore is complex and micro level treatment is not possible and fluid continue approach is used for analysis the concept of the representative volume (REV) which is used for analyzing the flow of fluid in porous bed. The REV is an assembly of many molecules contained in small volume. It is size should be much larger than the mean free path of single molecule and should be sufficiently small as compared to fluid domain such that the averaging fluid and flow properties are contained in, the bulk fluid properties will be obtained.

3.4 MOMENTUM EQUATION

The major modes of heat transfer consider as conduction and convection. The lab scale experiment is performed to calculating the various parameters at different boundary conditions. The fluid flows through the pores provided intense mixing of fluid and spreading in longitudinal and transverse directions. The flow past solid particles provides additional resistance to flow in additional to fluid – fluid resistance as in place flow extension of the Darcy to account for the presence of a wall inertia and viscous effect in the fluid phase and vortex formation in the poses called non Darcy effects. By accounting these factors the governing equations for the flow called the momentum equation (Hsu and Cheng 1990) is considered as

$$\rho \left[\frac{1}{\varepsilon} \frac{\partial U}{\partial t} + \frac{1}{\varepsilon} U . \nabla \left(\frac{U}{\varepsilon} \right) \right] = -\nabla p - \frac{\mu}{K} U + \frac{\mu}{\varepsilon \rho} \nabla^2 U - \frac{\rho}{K^{0.5}} f U |U| \qquad (3.2)$$

Where,

ρ= Density of fluid   K= Permeability of porous medium

μ= Dynamic viscosity   U= Darcy velocity

ε= Porosity of medium

And the factors,

$\frac{1}{\varepsilon} \frac{\partial U}{\partial t}$= Unsteady change in velocity $\frac{1}{\varepsilon} U . \nabla \left(\frac{U}{\varepsilon} \right)$= Change in velocity w.r.t. distance

∇p= Pressure gradient $\frac{\mu}{K} U$ = Darcy resistance

$\frac{\mu}{\varepsilon \rho} \nabla^2 U$ = Fluid-fluid viscous resistance $\frac{\rho}{K^{0.5}} f U |U|$= Forcheimmer drag

The fluid flows through a constant wall channel and the effects such as local thermal non-equilibrium and Nusselt number will be investigated by the equation(Wakao and Kaguei 1982):

$$Nu_p = 2 + 1.1 \ Pr^{0.33} Re_p^{0.6} \qquad (3.3)$$

Where Pr is Prandtl number, and Re_p is Reynolds number based on particle size

3.5 ENERGY EQUATION

As the hot fluid flows through the porous media it gives outs its energy to the solids phase and when the cold fluid flows through hot solid material in opposite direction, it retrieves the energy due to existence of the thermal non equilibrium. The heat transfer in the fluid solvent phase is calculated by the energy equation (Hsu 1999& Nakayama 2001) considered as

$$Fluid: \ \varepsilon (\rho C p)_f \left(\frac{\partial T}{\partial t} + u \frac{\partial T}{\partial x} \right) = k_{\text{eff}.f} \frac{\partial^2 T}{\partial x^2} + Q_{f \leftarrow s} \qquad (3.4)$$

$$\text{Solid: } (1 - \varepsilon)(\rho Cp)_s \frac{\partial T}{\partial t} = k_{\text{eff.s}} \frac{\partial^2 T}{\partial x^2} + Q_{f \to s} \qquad (3.5)$$

ε= Porosity of the medium   T= Temperature

ρ= Density   t= Time

Cp= Specific heat   k= Thermal conductivity

u= Velocity   Q= Inter phase heat transfer

f= Fluid phase   s= Solid phase

The effective thermal conductivity of fluid and solid phases in both the direction will be found out by the equations(Wakao 1979& Kague 1982)

$$\text{Longitudinal Direction: } k_{eff,f_z} = \varepsilon k_f + 0.5 Pe k_f \qquad (3.6)$$

$$\text{Transverse Direction: } k_{eff,f_r} = \varepsilon k_f + 0.1 Pe k_f \qquad (3.7)$$

Where k= Thermal conductivity ε= Porosity of the medium

Pe= Peclet number

3.6 HEAT ENERGY STORAGE AND RETRIEVAL

Hot fluid enters the porous domain from one of its ends for particular time called hot half cycle time ($t_p/2$) and cold fluid enters through the opposite end for cold half cycle time ($t_p/2$). Hence the total time period for the cycle is t_p. The frequency is measured by equation $2w/t_p$. As the temperature rises in the hot phase and decreases in the cold phase, the energy stored can be calculated but integration of solid and fluid phase temperature of length of bed for particular point of times gives the energy level. The stored energy in the particular hot phase is evaluated by difference of energy level between start and end of hot phase by the equation as mentioned as:

$$E_{\text{stored}} = E_{\text{in}} \_ E_{\text{out}} \qquad (3.8)$$

$$E_{stored} = \int_0^{t_p/2} (\rho c_p)_f u \sin(\omega t) \pi R^2 (T_{hot} - T_{cold})_{z=0} \, dt$$

$$- \int_0^{t_p/2} (\rho c_p)_f u \sin(\omega t) \pi R^2 (T - T_{cold})_{z=L} \, dt \qquad (3.9)$$

$$E_{retrieved} = E_{out} \_ E_{in} \qquad (3.10)$$

$$E_{retrieved} = \int_{t_p/2}^{t_p} (\rho c_p)_f u \sin(\omega t) \pi R^2 (T - T_{cold})_{z=0} \, dt$$

$$- \int_{t_p/2}^{t_p} (\rho c_p)_f u \sin(\omega t) \pi R^2 (T_{cold} - T_{cold})_{z=L} \, dt \qquad (3.11)$$

By considering the above equation the amount of heat transfer in solid – liquid phases can be calculated. The energy stored in hot phase and energy retrieved by the fluid phase can be calculated.

3.7 NONDIMENSIONALISATION OF PARAMETERS

The most convenient method of analyzing the result is by non dimensional parameters and the result becomes independent of individual parameters. The non-dimensionalisation of these parameters is suggested by Seo Yong Kim. The temperature is frequently used parameters for various calculations of thermal results in porous media. If T_h is temperature of hot fluid, T_c is temperature of cold fluid and T is instant temperature of fluid. The non dimensional value of temperature lies between zeros to one. Its Value can be determined by equation:

$$T_{Non\,dimensional} = \frac{T - T_c}{T_h - T_c} \qquad (3.12)$$

The value of time can be converted into non dimensional value by the flowing equation. If α is diffusivity of fluid, R is radius of bed tube and t is instant temperature then value of non Dimensional time is given by equation:

29

$$t_{\text{non dimensional}} = \alpha t/R \qquad\qquad (3.13)$$

In the porous bed the value of distance of thermocouple from inflow is very important and used for analyzing the thermal behavior. If x is the distance of flow and R is radius of bed tube then non dimensional distance is given by equation:

$$Z_{\text{non dimensional}} = x/R \qquad\qquad 9(3.14)$$

3.8 FREQUENCY OF PULSATION

The variation of temperature in porous bed alternatively changing the output temperature of porous bed is the frequency response of porous bed in which the temperature fluctuates between peaks and valleys. The maximum fluctuation of temperature is at hot domain. At the downstream the fluctuation reduces with the distance. The time period of the pulsation is the time gap accusing between successive peaks and valleys in response curve. The temperature rises to peak value shows the hot phase and decrease from peak to valleys is cold phase shown in frequency response curve drawn between temperature and time. The frequency response in porous bed is the function of forcing frequency defined as

$$\omega = 2\pi/t_p \qquad\qquad (3.15)$$

The reference frequency for every experiment for hot and cold pulsation the travel entire length of porous bed flowing at average speed in terms of time is defined as

$$\omega_{ref} = \frac{2\pi}{t_p} \qquad\qquad (3.16)$$

Where (tp) ref =2L /Average flow speed

$\qquad$ =2LR /Pe.α

Where L is length of porous bed, R is radius of profile.

Reference Frequency $\omega_{ref} = \dfrac{\pi Pe\,\alpha}{ZR^2}$

Dimensionless reference frequency

$\omega_{ref} = \dfrac{\pi Pe}{Z}$ where Z is non dimensional length of bed.

3.9 FRONT AMPLITUDE

The temperature in the oscillating is fluctuating from minimum to maximum values. During the hot phase the temperature rises to the maximum value and it falls to minimum value in cold phase. The curve is like a sine wave. The difference between maximum and minimum temperature at a location is known as amplitude. The temperature at hot domain is very high and decreases with downstream. Temperature at cold domain is low and increases with distances. The decrease in maximum temperature and increase in minimum temperature results fall in amplitude is known as attenuation.

3.10 FRONT SPEED

The front speed and front spread are used to measure the diffusive and advective transport property in porous medium. The front speed is measured for 0.5 degree temperature rise between two locations. It is spatial distance between given locations divided by difference in time taken by fluid to reach a temperature of 0.5 at each location. The non dimensional value is calculated by equation.

$$\text{Front speed} = \frac{\Delta Z}{Pe\,\Delta t} \qquad (3.17)$$

Where Pe is Peclet Number Δz is the distance between locations for the rise of 0.5 temperatures in Δt time. The front speed is the speed at which the thermal front travels in the bed. It is different from true fluid speed.

3.11 FRONT SPREAD

Front spread is the spread of fluid particles in different directions. In this the fluid particles spread in longitudenal and transverse direction. For the higher dispersion and heat loss higher is the front spread. The front spread at particular location indicates the role of difussion in heat energy transfer. It is measured for the fluid temperature to rise from 0.25 to 0.75 at the location. The non dimensional value of front spread is calculated by the equation as given:

$$\text{Front Spread} = (\Delta t)\, Pe \qquad\qquad (3.18)$$

Where Pe is Peclet Number and Δt is the time to rise from 0.25 to 0.75.

The front spread is function of Pe, higher the value of Pe, the higher is the front spread.

3.12 PHASE LAG

The rise of temperature in oscillating flow of porous media occurs after some time gap at upstream locations. The occurrence of maximum and minimum temperature after a time gap is known as phase lag. The phase lag depends upon the time period of pulsation. For smaller time period the phase lag is larges where as for long time period the phase lag is smaller. The non dimensional value of phase lag is obtained by multiplying a factor

$$\text{Phase Lag} = 2\alpha/\omega Z \qquad\qquad (3.19)$$

Where Z is distance between two locations

3.13 SPECIFIC SURFACE AREA

During the flow of fluid in porous media, there is intense mixing of fluid with solid particle surface. The heat energy exchange between solid and liquid phase depend upon the surface area of solid material. In these experiments the various particle size of solid materials are considered and surface area changes according to size. If ϵ is porosity of porous bed and d_p particle diameter then specific surface area A_{if} is expresses by equation (Dullion 1979) as given below:

$$A_{if} = \frac{6(1-\varepsilon)}{d_p} \qquad (3.20)$$

Non dimensional value of Specific Area

$$A_f = \frac{6(1-\varepsilon)R}{d_p} \qquad (3.21)\text{Where R is the radius of pipe.}$$

CHAPTER 4

EXPERIMENTAL SET UP

4.1 INTRODUCTION

An experimental set up is fabricated to evaluate the thermal storage effects of porous domain subjected to hot and cold fluid flows. When the hot fluid flows through an initially cold domain, the response is called step response but when hot and cold fluid flows alternately the response is frequency response. The above flow is called oscillatory flow.

The thermal properties of solid phase of porous bed are shown in Table 4.1, the fluid phase being water. Steel spherical ball have high thermal conductivity (k) and low specific heat (Cp) than there of glass. The thermal front is expected to be quite different for the two cases.

Table 4.1: Thermal properties of glass and steel

Solid Phase	Density, ρ [Kg/m^3]	Thermal Storage Capacity, ρCp [KJ/m^{3}K]	Thermal Conductivity, k [W/m K]
Steel	9288	3768.3	14.9
Glass	2595	1869	1.09

Further in this chapter the details of experimental setup, the components comprising the experimental setup and the measuring devices with the specification are discussed.

4.2 FREQUENCY RESPONSE OF POROUS BED

The important component of the experiment is porous bed. The Figure 4.1(a) shows the physical model of porous bed in which the hot fluid is passed through the initially cold bed (at room temperature) through one end and exit through the other end, where as the cold fluid enters through the other end and exhausted to the end in which the hot fluid enters.

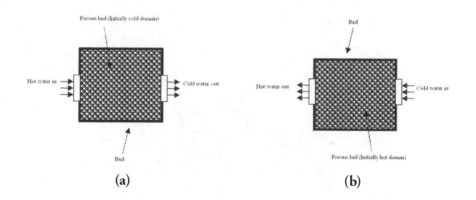

(a)   (b)

Figure 4.1: (a) Flow of hot fluid in porous bed
(b) Flow of cold fluid in porous bed

In this experimentation the porous bed is initially saturated with cold water and saves the minimum temperature at any location in the porous bed. The Figure 4.1(b) shows the step response of porous bed in which the hot fluid passes through initially cold bed and temperature at any point is the function of the time.

At non dimensional distance Z=0, temperature is maintained at unit value. This can be expressed in dimensionless form as

$$T(z,r,t) = 0 \text{ where } 0 \leq z \leq L \text{ and } 0 \leq r \leq R \text{ for } t \leq 0 \qquad (4.1)$$

In a step response the hot water is introduced through the inlet plain for all times and can be expressed as

$$T(0,r,t) = 1 \text{ for } t > 0$$

In the frequency response, the hot and cold fluid flows alternately in the opposite direction for the equal time. The time through which the hot fluid flows is known as hot phase and the time through which the cold fluid flows is known as cold phase. The sum of the hot phase and cold phase is known as time period.

The Figure 4.2 shows the frequency response of porous bed and temperature is function of time. The maximum and minimum level of temperature during the experimentation is slightly less than the hot temperature but more than the cold fluid temperature as shown in the Figure.

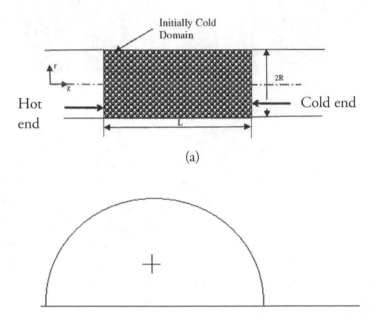

(a)

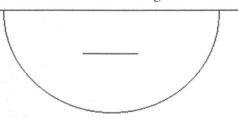

(b) Hot phase: Hot water enters through hot end and leaves through cold end

(c) Cold phase: Cold waters enters through cold
end and leaves through cold end

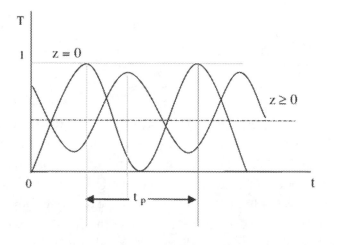

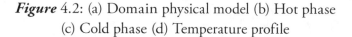

(d) Temperature profile at z = 0, z > 0

Figure 4.2: (a) Domain physical model (b) Hot phase
(c) Cold phase (d) Temperature profile

The initial condition for the problem is expressed in equation (4.1) and the boundary condition can be written as

Hot Phase $T(o,r,t) = 1$ $o < t \leq t_{p/2}$

Cold Phase $T(L,r,t) = 0$ $t_{p/2} < t \leq t_p$

4.3 REQUIREMENTS FOR EXPERIMENTAL SET UP

The experimental set up should be accurate and sensitive so that it can achieve the desired results within the given boundary conditions. The most important component of experiment is porous bed, in which the tube should be insulated properly and material of tube should have less thermal conductivity to avoid loss of heat. The spherical glass or steel beads should be closely packed. The flow of fluid should be fully saturated and maintained at a constant head. The hot water temperature should be maintained a constant temperature using immersion heater and temperature controller. The separate storage tanks are required for the hot and cold fluids. The pumping system should be used for supplying the water from storage tanks to the constant head tanks. The flow measuring device is required to measure the rate of flow. For the temperature measurement in the bed the thermocouples should be inserted in the porous bed. The temperature measurement and recording devices should be sensitive. For this the thermocouple should be connected with the data acquisition system for converting the signal from analog to digital form and interfaced with PC for recording the data permanently. The system should be able to store the complete experimentation records. The experimental set up and PC should be earthed properly. The flow should be continuous, without air trap and leakage. The diameter of the porous bed tube should be at least ten times the diameter of the bead so that the wall effects on the velocity profiles are low. The constant head fluid tanks should have continuous display of temperature in porous bed and some initial length should be considered as a settling length for the flow and the thermocouples should be inserted, similarly the temperature near the end of bed should be avoided for minimize the end effects on temperature measurements.

4.4 MAIN COMPONENTS

4.4.1 Porous Bed

The porous bed is the most important component of the experimental set up. It consists of a pipe, which is made of insulating material and covered again with insulating materials. To avoid heat loss PVC pipe is used in this experiment with pressure capacity of 6.0 Kg/m^2 and wrapped with insulating material. The internal diameter of pipes is 84 mm and thickness of pipe material is 3.22 mm. The total length of the pipe is 66 cm which have the total volume for the fluid and beads as 3.658 Liters. The glass or steel balls are closely packed in PVC pipe. The diameter of steel or glass balls is to be less than 8.4 mm. to ensure that the diameter of pipe is ten times the diameter of bead. The PVC pipe, constant head tanks and storage tanks are fitted on iron pipe table. The constant head tanks are positioned at such a height that head of 115 cm is maintained. Five thermocouples are inserted at a distance of 90 mm from each other and distance of 150 mm is left at both ends to avoid end effects as shown in Figure 4.3.

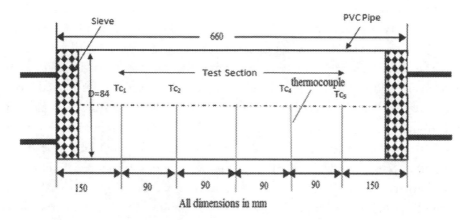

Figure 4.3: Porous bed

The whole system and table is grounded to avoid excessive voltage to thermcouple and protect high sensitive data acquisition card. A pipe of 12.5 mm diameter pipe is used to supply the water to bed from constant head tank. The hot water pipe to the bed is covered with insulating material to avoid heat loss. The distances of the thermocouples and their coresponding non dimensional distance calculated by equation X/R (where X is distance and R is radius of pipe) from the inflow plane is mentioned in Table 4.2

Table 4.2: Location of thermocouples from
hot inflow plane and corresponding non dimensional distances

Thermocouple No	Location of thermocouple from hot water inflow to bed in mm	Non-dimensional distance of thermocouple from hot water inflow to bed Z
1	150	0
2	240	2.1
3	330	4.3
4	420	6.4
5	510	8.6

Three different types of beads are used as solid media in experimentation. In the first type of experimentation, the steel balls of 4.55 mm diameter are filled in pipe. The balls are closely packed and care is taken while filling so that the thermocouple wires are not damaged. The water is supplied with outlet valve closed so that the air is completely removed and saturated flow is maintained. In the second type of experimentation the glass balls of 6.5 mm diameter are used as solid media. As the thermal conductivity of glass material is less than the steel. The temperature rises sharply in glass beads as compared to steel beads. In third type of experimentation the steel balls of 6.5 mm diameter are used. The flow rate is maintained between 1.5 to 2.5 lpm. As the Reynolds no based on R in each experiment is above 200, so the flow is considered as turbulent flow.

4.4.2 Thermocouple

The temperature in the porous bed is measured by thermocouples. It is an instrument, which converts temperature gradient to Millivolts. Thermocouples used in this experimentation are K type (Chromel–Alumel material) [Chromel is 90% nickel & 10% chromium and Alumel is 95% nickel, 2%manganese, 2% aluminum & 1% silicon]. It has the sensitivity of 41µV/C with the measuring range from -200 to 1250^0 C. The thicknesses of wire are 1.6 mm and develop 10 mV per degree centigrade rise. It has two wires and length of wire is one meter.

4.4.3 Thermocouple Cold Junction Compensation Circuit

The thermocouples are very sensitive and will have certain temperature response time. The thermocouples are connected to signal conditioner and temperature compensation circuit. As the thermocouple is sensitive to temperature difference, the temperature of reference junction must be known to make a temperature measurement. One way to measure the accurate temperature is to keep the reference junction at ice bath. This has advantage of zero output voltage at zero degrees centigrade. A more convenient approach known as cold junction compensation circuit is to add a compensatory voltage to thermocouple output so that the reference junction appears to be at 0^0 C independent of actual temperature. The IC LM 335 which has linear voltage-temperature relation is used in the compensation circuit. It operates to the perpetual voltage at absolute temperature of 10 mV/degree Celsius. In a single supply circuit resistance R_3 and R_4 divide down the 10mV/ degree Celsius output of IC LM335 to match the See back coefficient of the thermocouple. The LM329 and its associate voltage divider provide a voltage to buck out the zero degree Celsius output of the LM335. The resistance R_1 and R_2 can be adjusted so that V1-V2 is equal to the thermocouple output voltage at known ambient temperature. The complete circuit with resistances and IC is described in the Figure 4.4. The circuit has the feasibility of periodic calibrations with the help of simple a multi meter.

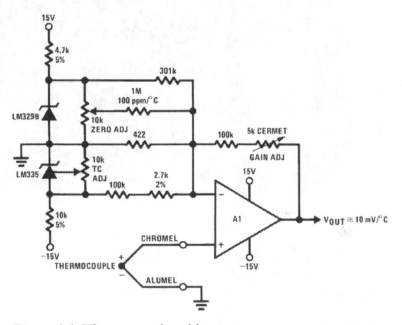

Figure 4.4: Thermocouple cold junction compensation circuit

4.4.4 Data Acquisition Card

The output of cold junction compensation circuit is in analog signal form, which is required to be converted into digital signal form. Data acquisition card (DAQ card) converts the analog signal into digital signal in PC. AD LINK 2213 DAQ card is used in this experimentation, which is high performance, multifunction card. It can sample up to 16 analog input channels with different gain setting. Multiple DAQ 2213 card can be synchronized interface (SSI) bus. DAQ card is connected with cold junction compensation circuit by 68 pin VHDCI connector (Squeezy cable). ADDLINK provides the driver for LAB VIEW software. As per the user guide and instruction manual supplied with card, the DAQ card is installed in PC and 8.2 version LAB VIEW software is loaded. The system was programmed as per the requirement of five thermocouples and temperature readings in the digital form are recorded. DAQ card is so sensitive that it records five readings in one second and up to ten decimal numbers.

Figure 4.5: 2213 AD Link Data Acquisition Card

4.4.5 Rotameter

Flow rate is measured by a rotameter fitted on exit side of porous bed. Glass material vertical type rotameter is used which is having capacity of 5 liters per minute. Rotameter is fitted with adjusting knob, so that the flow can be adjusted as per the desired flow rate. The accuracy of rotameter is assured measuring water in measuring beaker for one minute.

4.4.6 Constant Head Tank

Separate constant head tanks are used for hot and cold water in experimentation. The tanks are fixed on a table so that constant head of 1150 mm is maintained. Tanks have three connections, one inlet and two outlets.

Pump from storage tank supply water to constant head tank through inlet connection. One outlet connection supply water to porous bed and other for overflow to storage tank. Capacity of each tank is 20 Litters. Immersion heater is fitted to the hot water tank with thermostat so that constant temperature water is supplied to porous bed.

4.4.7 Storage Tank

Storage tanks are provided to avoid wastage of water and maintain the level of water in constant head tank. It can store large quantity of water. A pump is provided in each storage tank to supply water to constant head tank. Pump can supply water to height of 2.8 m with power input 40 watts and can supply 3800 lph. The over flow provided in each tank maintain constant level of water.

4.4.8 Hot Water Flow

The hot water flows to porous bed from the constant head. The constant head tank of 20 Liters capacity is used and the constant head to 1150 mm is maintained. Immersion heater is inserted in constant head tank with temperature controller. Water is supplied to porous bed at constant temperature and constant flow rate. Temperature gauge is provided in constant head tank to show the temperature of hot water continuously. The layout of the hot water circuit is shown in Figure 4.6.

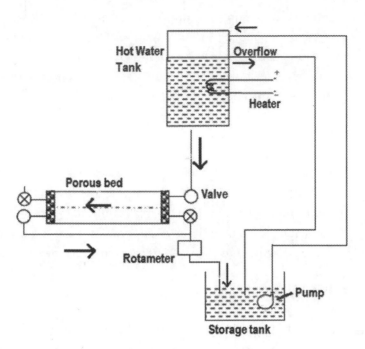

Figure 4.6: Hot water circuit

4.4.9 Cold Water Flow: The cold fluid used is as normal water. The cold water flows in a direction opposite to the direction of hot water. The valves are used to control the direction of flow. The cold water flows from the constant head tank of 20 Litters capacities. The pump used for the flow is 40 watt power with maximum head of 2.8 m and output 3800 lph. Thermometer gauge is provided in constant head tank to show temperature of constant head water continuously. The layout of cold water circuit is shown if Figure 4.7.

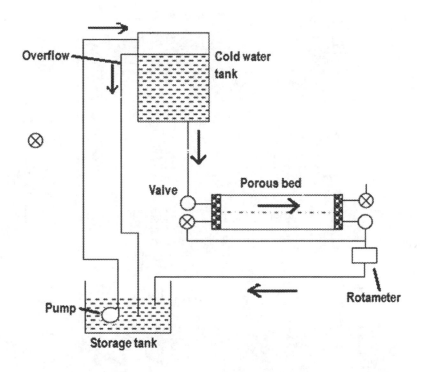

Figure 4.7: Cold water circuit

4.5 APPRATUS LAYOUT AND EXPERIMENT PROCEDURE

The layout of apparatus is shown in Figure 4.8. Each component fitted in appratus is named as shown in the figure. The flow of water is controlled by valves fitted in inlet and outlet side of porous bed. The water flows from constant head tank to porous bed and discharged to respective storage tank through rotameter. Thermometers are inserted in hot and cold water tank for continous control of temperature. Thermocouples inserted in porous bed detects the temperature and is reorded in the PC through cold junction circuit and data acquisition card.

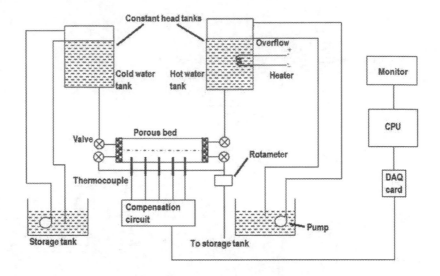

Figure 4.8: Apparatus layout

Figure 4.9: Photograph of experimental set up

4.5.1 Experimental Procedure

Experiment procedure involves initial warming up of system, checking of various components for leakage and functioning. It also involve grounding of equipments, availability of constant voltage supply and required water supply. As per the DAQ card instructions the system is to be switched on at least 15 minutes before taking any observation. The system is switched on along with cold junction compensatory circuit for 30 minutes. The cold water is supplied to porous bed with exit valve closed to remove air from the porous bed. It ensures the suitabilities of the bed. After complete warming up operation the procedure for experimentation is as follows:

- Switch on the hot and cold pumps.
- Open the cold water exit valve.
- Adjust rotameter for desired flow rate and record reading.
- Switch on imersion heater fixed in hot water tank.
- Set the thermostat to required temperature of hot water.
- Set the PC as per requirement and log on LAB VIEW, it will automatically log with DAQ card.
- Set the timing accordingly, for step response hot water would flow for long time and for frequency response hot & cold water flows alternately for equal time. The opening and closing of valves should be at same time so that the flow rate through them is same.
- Moniter the temperature of hot and cold water in PC.
- When the temperature of hot water becomes constant then start the programe and open the hot & cold valves alternately to obtain oscillatory response.
- Record the temperature data for atleast six set of readings.
- The data is recorded in PC. After the experiment is over, stop the programe. then log off LAB VIEW.
- Close all the valves.
- Switch off heater and pumps.
- Switch off the main supply.
- Analyse the result for further calcultions.

4.6 ACCURACY

Accuracy is most important for true value of reading. All the component before fittment to the appratus were checked for correctness. The components purchesed from varias sources are calibrated before dispatch. Thermocouples were calibrated with lab heater kit and cold junction compensation circuit were calibarated separately. Reading of cold water temperature from PC is compared with temperature gauge fitted on cold water tank, which confirms the accuracy of whole system. The accuracy is checked by comparing the results with results of [7].

4.7 REPEATABILITY

Repeatability also attributes the important role in experimentation. This refers to the value of correctness for number of measurements. The repeatability can be ensured by comparing same input value to the system. If the system gives the same output then system is considered as accurate.

4.8 REPEATABILITY PROCEDURE

In this apparatus the controls input is flow rate which is adjusted in rotameter. The dimension less expression of flow rate is Reynold's number. Further convinient way to express nondimensional flow rate is by Peclet number. The repeatability is examined at different Peclet number with various hot water temperature. The non dimensional temperature is calculated by the equations as mentioned in Chapter 3.

4.9 REPEATABILITY OF FREQUENCY RESPONSE EXPERIMENTS

4.9.1 Steel Water Bed-I

The repeatability of steel water bed I is checked at different flow rate and different hot and cold temperatures. In this steel bed the solid material is spherical steel beds of d_p = 4.55 mm. The experiments are carried out at different flow rates of Pe =1287, 1202, 1158. The temperature of hot water is different at each flow rate. The difference of hot and cold water is also different in every experiment. The following parameters are considered while checking the repeatability of frequency response.

***Table* 4.3**: Details of parameter related to repeatability of steel water bed I

Sr. No.	Peclet number.	Flow rate lpm	Reynolds number	Time for hot/cold Flow sec	Diff. bet hot/cold temp. in ^{0}C
1.	1287	1.5	236	90	14.7
2.	1202	1.4	220	90	19.2
3.	1158	1.35	212	90	17.5

The temperature profiles are plotted for the different flow rate at locations Z=0. The profile for the hot phase and cold phase are shown in Figure 4.10 & 4.11 for hot phase and cold phase at Pe= 1287, 1202 & 1158.

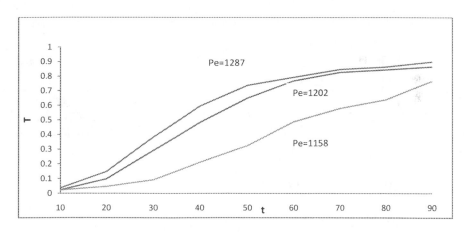

***Figure* 4.10:** Hot phase in steel water bed d_p= 4.55 mm at Pe= 1287,1202 & 1158

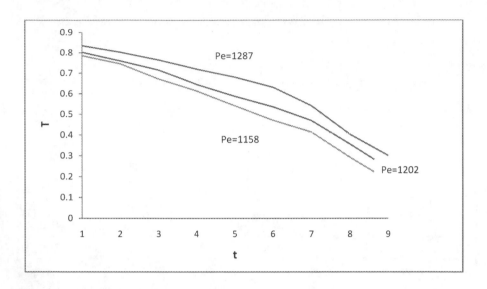

Figure *4.11:* Cold phase in steel water bed
d_p=4.55 mm at Pe= 1287,1202 & 1158

Table 4.4: Details of temparature for repeatability of steel water bed I

Peclet number	T hot in ^{0}C	T cold in ^{0}C	Frequency (rad/s)
1287	49.7	35	0.0349
1202	50.2	31	0.0349

4.9.2 Repeatability of Glass Water Bed

The repeatability of glass water bed is chekched by varing the flow rate at different hot and cold water temperature. In the galss water bed the glass spherical beads of d_p = 6.5 mm are closely packed in porous bed. The flow rate is maintained at Pe= 2054, 1629 & 1542. The following parameters are consider for checking the repeatability of the glass water bed.

Table 4.5: Details of parameter related to repeatability of glass water bed

S. no.	Peclet number	Flow rate lpm	Reynolds number	Frequency rad/S	Difference of hot & cold water Temp. in ^{0}C
1	1629	1.9	299	0.0349	23.4
2	2054	2.4	377	0.0349	24.2
3	1542	1.8	283	0.0349	20.8

As the thermal conductivity of glass is less the temperature rises sharply in the hot phase and falls sharply in the cold phase. The temperature profiles are different from steel water bed. The profiles of different flow rate are plotted in Figures 4.12 & 4.13 at location Z=0.

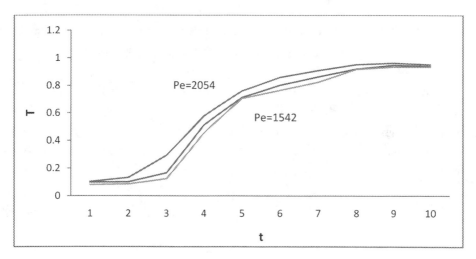

Figure *4.12:* Temperature profile of glass water bed in hot phase at *Pe =2054, 1629 & 1542*

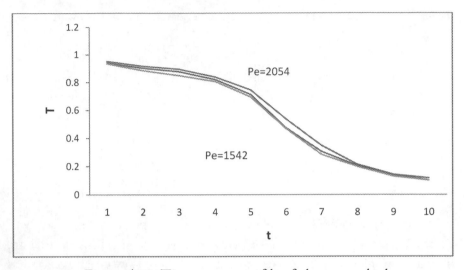

Figure 4.13: Temperature profile of glass water bed
in cold phase at *Pe* =2054, 1629 & 1542

As the thermal conductivity of glass is less the temperature rises sharply in the hot phase and falls sharply in the cold phase. The temperature profiles are different from steel water bed.

The temperature profile of thermocouple at location Z=0 shows similar trends but increased rise rate. The temperature at this location rises sharply than the temperature at the end location Z= 8.6. The thermocouple Z= 4.3 located at the middles. The rate of rise is less at Z= 4.3 and decreases with distance.

4.9.3 Steel water Bed-II

The procedure for checking the repeatability is same as in case of steel water bed and glass water bed. In this water bed the steel balls of 6.5 mm diameter are closely packed. The repeatability tests are carried out at different flow rate with different hot water temperature. The profiles of different location thermocouples are platted. The curves of thermocouple near the hot water domain rises sharply than the thermocouple near the cold water domain. The frequency of flow is kept at 0.0349. The following parameter are considers for checking the repeatability of the steel water bed II.

Table 4.6: Details of parameter related to repeatability of steel water bed II

Sr. no.	Peclet number	Flow rates lpm	Reynolds number	Frequency (rad/s)	Diff. b/w hot & cold water beds in ^{0}C
1	1888	2.0	346	0.0349	23
2	1542	1.8	283	0.0349	15.3
3	1368	1.6	251	0.0349	22

The hot and cold water temperature are maintained as described in the table. The rise of temperature is very smooth. The maximum temperature is observed at Z=0 location and at Z=8.6 location the rise of temperature is very low which indicates that maximum heat energy is absorbed during the flow in the bed.

4.10 CLOSURE

The complete apparatus and each instrument mentioned in this chapter is expected to generate the correct value during the experimentation. The standard results can be obtained by analyzing the correct values. The components are purchased from the various sources and from various locations. The data acquisition card was properly calibrated before despotched from the USA. Each component were calibrated individualy in the institute labs. The cold junction compensatory circuit is self febricated in the institude and calibrated with the heater kit and multimeter in the institute. The experimental set up and system including DAO card is safeguarded against excesssive voltage. The voltage emitted in thermocouple is due to the seeback effect only. The DAQ card installation and saftware loading were as per the manuals provided with DAO cord.

The hot water temperature for each experiment were controlled. The repeatability of the experimental set up were found satisfactory. At last the experimental set up provide repeatable and reliable results which can be used for the analysis.

CHAPTER 5

FREQUENCY RESPONSE OF STEEL WATER BED-I

5.1 INTRODUCTION

The frequency response of a steel water bed having closely packed spherical steel balls of diameter 4.55 mm is discussed in this chapter, the oscillating fluid being water. The oscillating flow is different than plain and pulsating flow as the direction of the hot and the cold water flow is opposite. In pulsating flow, the hot and the cold water flows from the same end but alternately whereas in oscillating flow it flows alternately but through the opposite ends. Table 4.1 and 5.1 show the thermo-physical properties of steel and water respectively. Using these values, the Thermo-physical properties of steel water bed are calculated and shown in Table 5.2. The porosity of steel bed-I is measured as 0.435. The tube to the particle ratio is quite large for flat velocity profile in the bed. The total length of bed is 660 mm used for experimentation. A bed length of 300 mm is used to minimize the end and the entrance effects. As the water flows through the two ends alternately; the flow development effects in hot water flow becomes end effects during the cold water flow as it reveres its direction. The thermal non-equilibrium between the solid and the fluid phases is a key for thermal response of porous bed. It is calculated experimentally and compared with those of other researchers [Kuznetsov]. The flow of the hot and the cold water through the opposite ends creates a sine wave type pulses in the porous bed as shown in Figure 5.1 which is similar to those of the thermal non-equilibrium.

Table 5.1: Thermal physical properties of water

Density, ρ [kg/ m^3]	Specific heat c_p [J/(kg.k)]	Thermal conductivity, k [W/(m.k)]	Kinematic viscosity, ν [m^2/s]	Thermal Diffusivity [m^2/s]
995.7	4178	0.61	0.802x10^{-6}	0.146x10^{-6}

Table 5.2: Thermo-physical properties of steel water bed-I

Thermal capacity ratio $\beta=\dfrac{(\rho c_p)_f}{(\rho c_p)_s}$	Thermal conductivity ratio $\lambda=\dfrac{(k)_f}{(k)_s}$	Particle diameter dp (mm)	Tube to particle ratio D/d$_p$	Specific surface area, A$_f$ m^2/m^3
1.1	0.04	4.55	18.46	744.23

5.2 FREQUENCY RESPONSE AND CYCLIC TEMPERATURE PROFILES

The cyclic temperature profile for frequency response of steel water bed I are discussed in this section. The layout of the porous bed is shown in Figure 4.7 and position of thermocouples is also shown in the figure. In oscillating flow the hot and cold fluid enters alternately from the opposite ends. In hot plane the entrance effects are seen on left position of bed, where as in cold plain on right side. As the hot fluid enters through hot end in an initially cold domain, the temperature rises at various locations as in case of step response [7]. After the hot phase time period the cold water enters from other end and temperature falls at various location. As the hot water flows again, it raises the temperature at various locations in the bed from the minimum temperature of first cycle. The maximum temperature increases in the each cycle. The increase of maximum temperature in every cycle is known as unsteady state.

The frequency response of steel bed- I are obtained at the various flow rates and different inlet hot water temperature by keeping the difference of the hot and cold water temperature. The cyclic temperature profile in steel water bed is analyzed at three flow rate *Pe*= 1158, 1202 and 1287 and t$_p$ is 180 seconds, thereby hot and cold phase time is 90 seconds both. Hence the oscillating frequency is *0.034 rad/s*. The variation of temperature with locations at various locations at three flow rate is shown in Figures 5.1, 5.2 and 5.3.

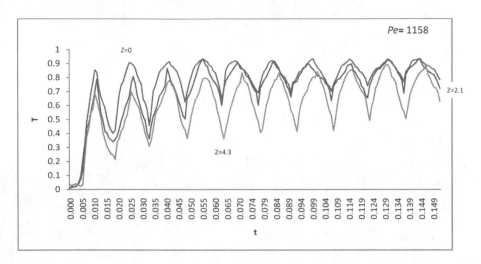

(a)

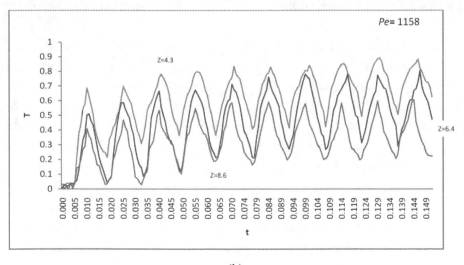

(b)

***Figure** 5.1*: Temperature variation with time in steel water bed I d_p = 4.55 mm at (a) Z= 0, 2.1& 4.3 (b) *Z = 4.3, 6.4 & 8.6*, at *Pe = 1158 & ω = 0.034 rad/s*

The Figure 5.1 shows the cyclic temperature profile at all locations at flow rate Pe =1158. Figure 5.1(a) shows that at location Z = 0 nearer to hot inflow plane, the temperature rises to value of 0.83 in the first cycle and further increases to 0.91 after four cycles when the steady state is established. The temperature falls to value of 0.38 in first cycle and increases to 0.41 after three cycles. The temperature fluctuates between the values 0.91 to 0.41 in the steady state. The temperature remains highest at this location as the hot water enter the hot domain. At location Z = 2.1 the maximum temperature rises to a value of 0.78. At Z = 4.3 (midpoint) the maximum temperature reduces to 0.68 and minimum temperature falls to 0.22. The Figure 5.1(b) shows that at location Z = 8.6 the maximum temperature remains at minimum value 0.41 and increases to value o.52 in the steady state. The minimum temperature remains to value of 0.04 for three cycle. The temperature fluctuates between the lower value levels. As the hot water enters at Z = 0 end the heat energy absorbed at location Z = 0 is large as compared to location Z= 8.6. The difference between the peak value for Z = 4.3 and 6.4 is approaching closer after number of cycles. Peak values at the location Z = 8.6 is increasing at faster rate than location Z = 0. Temperature variation at Z = 8.6 location is more as compared to the location Z = 0. Hot water leaves with less energy due to lower peak temperature at exit end.

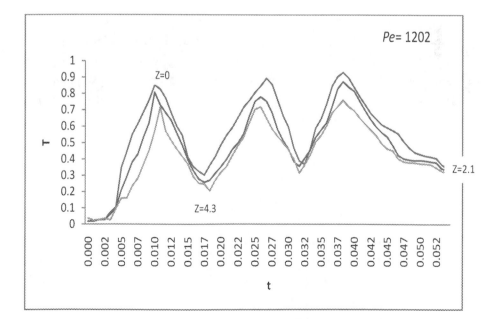

(a)

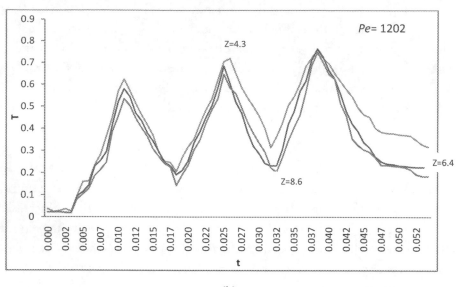

(b)

Figure *5.2*: Variation of temperature with time in
steel water bed d_p = 4.55 mm at (a) Z= 0, 2.1& 4.3
(b) *Z = 4.3, 6.4 & 8.6, at Pe =1202 & ω= 0.0349 rad/s*

The cyclic temperature profiles are shown in Figure 5.2 (a) & (b) at flow
rate *Pe* = 1202 at all five locations. The trends obtained are similar but the rise
of temperature is faster due to increase in flow rate. Figure 5.2 (a) shows that
the temperature at location Z = 0 rises to value of 0.85 and subsequent falls
to value of 0.30 in first cycle. The maximum temperature further increases
to value of 0.93 after thee cycles. At location Z = 2.1 the temperature rises to
a value of 0.80 which is higher than at *Pe* = 1158 and subsequently falls to
value of 0.30. The Figure 5.2 (b) shows the temperature profiles at locations
Z = 4.3, 6.4 & 8.6. As cold water enters from the location Z = 8.6 end the
peak temperature at location Z = 8.6 is quite low at value 0.51 as compared
to other locations but higher than flow rate *Pe* = 1158. Also the minimum
temperature is lower than the other locations to value 0.14. There is minimum
temperature rise at Z = 8.6 location and heat energy absorbed and retrieved is
low as compared to other locations. At location Z = 4.3 which is at mid point
the temperature rises to value of 0.70 value and falls to value of 0.16. Due to
increase in flow rate the maximum temperature rises to higher value and rate

of increase & decrease is faster. The fluctuation of temperature is at higher level at the hot domain as compared to cold domain.

The Figure 5.3 (a) and (b) shows the temperature profiles at *Pe* = 1287 at various locations. The Figure 5.3(a) shows that as the flow rate is increased the value of temperature at Z= 0 increases to 0.87 which is quite high than that of 0.83 at *Pe*= 1158 at same locations and subsequently falls to value of 0.28 in the cold phase. The temperature increases to 0.96 in three cycles and fluctuate at higher level between the values 0.96 and 0.46. At location Z = 2.1 the temperature rises to value of 0.83 and falls to 0.26. The Figure 5.3 (b) shows that at the cold end location Z= 8.6 the temperature rises to value of 0.53 which is lowest as compared to other locations due to location at the end of hot phase and most of the energy is absorbed by previous locations. The temperature falls to a value of 0.03 which is lower than at *Pe* = 1158. At location Z= 6.4 the temperature rises to a value of 0.61 and falls to 0.09 in cold phase. The minimum temperature remains at lower value at locations Z = 6.4 and 8.6 due to direction of water from opposite end. It is observed that rise of temperature is maximum at the hot domain and with the increase of flow rate the maximum temperature increases. The peak temperature does not remain for even short time at Z = 0. The maximum temperature decreases with the locations at all three flow rate

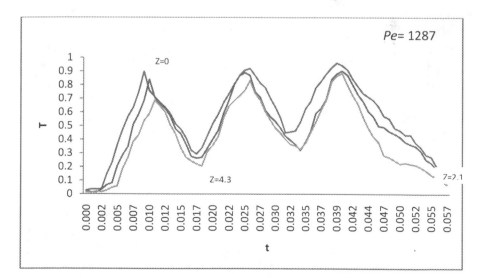

(a)

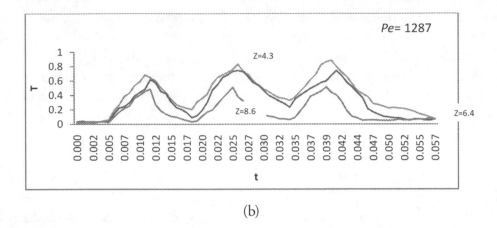

(b)

Figure 5.3: Variation of temperature with time in
steel water bed d_p = 4.55mm at (a) Z= 0, 2.1& 4.3
(b) *Z = 4.3, 6.4 & 8.6, at Pe =1287 ω= 0.0349 rad/s*

5.2.1 Maximum and Minimum Temperature

The pulsations in porous media oscillating flow are different from the pulsations in plane flow. The rise of temperature and fall of temperature is very sharp as compared to porous media in which there is no exchange of energy with solid phase. The temperature variation with the locations in steel bed- I at different time t= 0.011, 0.026 &0.067 is shown in Figure 5.4.

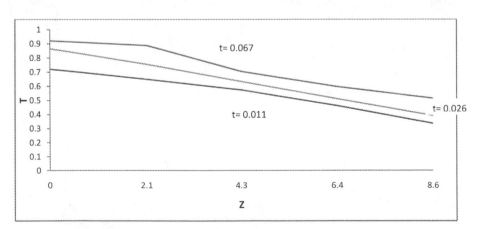

Figure 5.4: Variation of temperature with locations in steel
water bed d_p = 4.55mm at *Pe =1202 & ω=0.034 rad/s*

The value of peak temperature increases with the passage of time at particular locations and value of minimum temperature also increased with the passage of time which shows that the porous media retains some amount of energy at the end of the cold phase. At time t= 0.011 the maximum temperature at Z = 0 is 0.71 and reduces to 0.38 at Z = 8.6. As the time approaches the steady state t= 0.067 the value of temperature increases to 0.92. The peak value is increased in each cycle by some amount. The peak value decreases with the location and it is minimum at Z = 8.6.

In cold phase the cold fluid enters at cold domain, the cold fluid extract the energy and temperature of fluid increases with the distance. The temperature increases smoothly with distance. The Variation of the minimum temperature at time t= 0.018, 0.032 & 0.062 is shown in Figure 5.5

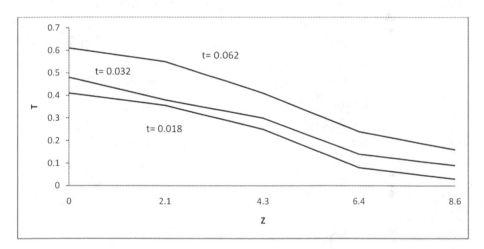

Figure *5.5*: Variation of valley temperature with locations in steel water bed d_p = 4.55mm time t= 0.018, 0.032 & 0.062 at *Pe =1202 & ω=0.034 rad/s*

It is observed that minimum temperature increases from cold domain towards hot domain. The temperature reaches to highest value at Z = 0 as the cold water retrieves the heat energy from porous media. The increase of temperature is low at time t=0.018 to value 0.41. At time t= 0.032 it increases to 0.48 and further increases to 0.61 value as the steady state is reached. It is concluded that minimum value increases with time and maximum at the hot domain. The value of temperature remains minimum at location Z= 8.6 due to entrance of cold water at cold domain.

5.3 FRONT AMPLITUDE VARIATION AND PHASE LAG

In oscillating flow temperature rises to maximum value in hot phase, where as it falls to minimum value in cold phase. The difference between maximum and minimum value of temperature is called front amplitude. In downstream locations the maximum temperature reduces and minimum temperature increases. The decrease in maximum temperature will reduce front amplitude at those locations. The decrease in amplitude of the temperature is called attenuation. The resulting temperature is reached when the amplitude of pulse falls to zero and temperature value lies between the hot phase temperature and cold phase temperature. The amplitude calculated at various locations is shown in bar chart Figure 5.6. The variation of amplitude with time at different locations at Pe= 1287, 1202 and 1158 is shown in the Figures 5.7 (a) and 5.8 (a) & (b).

The value of temperature in hot phase is not same at all location and the maximum temperature do not occur at the same time. The maximum value of temperature of different locations occurs at different time. The time gap between the maximum values of two locations is called phase lag, denoted by ϕ. The phase lag depend upon time period. Larger the time period will result smaller phase lag. The phase lag at Pe = 1287 is shown in Figure 5.7 (b) between locations.

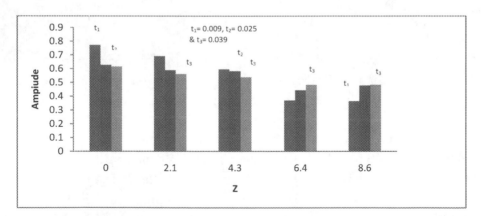

Figure *5.6:* Variation of amplitude with locations in steel water bed d_p = 4.55 mm at time t=0.009, 0.025 & 0.039 at Pe =1287and ω= *0.034 rad/s*

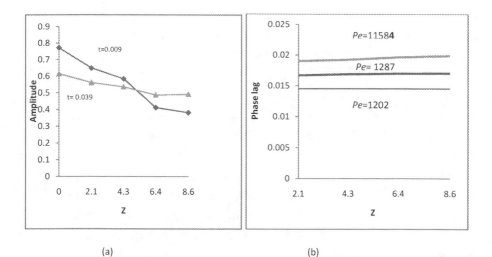

(a)   (b)

Figure *5.7:* Variation of (a) amplitude with location at *Pe =1287*
(b) phase lag at various locations in steel water bed d_p = 4.55 mm
at *Pe = 1158, 1202 & 1287and* ω= *0.034 rad/s*

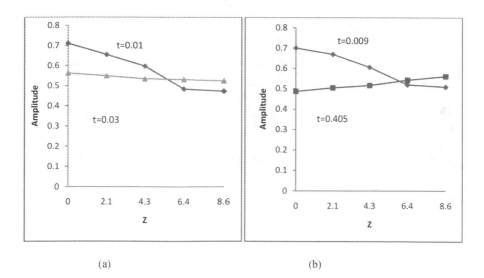

(a)   (b)

Figure *5.8:* Amplitude variation with locations at various locations in steel
water bed d_p = 4.55 mm at (a) *Pe =1202 (b) Pe=1158 at* ω= *0.034 rad/s*

The Figure 5.7 shows that at *Pe* = 1287, the value of amplitude is 0.78
at locations Z= 0 at initial time 0.009 which is highest being near to hot
domain. The amplitude decreases with the locations and at the location Z= 6.4

which is nearer to the cold domain decreases to value of 0.41. The amplitude decreases at locations Z = 0 at time t= 0.38 because 0f the increase of minimum temperature. The amplitude in the Z=6.4 increases to 0.48 due to increase in the higher temperature where as being nearer to cold domain the lower temperature is not much increasing. The increase and decrease in amplitude indicates that the total amount of energy absorbed is approximately same in all the cycles. As per the Figure 5.8 (a) the amplitude is higher at location Z= 0 of value 0.84 at *Pe* = 1202. It decreases sharply due to increase in lower temperature. The amplitude at the location Z=6.4 is increasing from the value of 0.50 to 0.58. The average amplitude will be same at all the locations. At *Pe* = 1158 the decrease in the amplitude at locations Z = 2.1 is at faster rate from 0.69 to 0.51. By comparing the amplitude at the three flow rate it is observed that at high flow rate the decrease in the amplitude is at low rate near the hot domain. At low flow rate the decrease in amplitude is at high rate. The amplitude of various locations approaches each other after three cycles in the steady state. The value of amplitude increases with increase in the flow rate.

It is obseved there is significant gap occure at peak temperature locations. The phase lag remains constant during the hot phase. The experiment is carried out at three flow rates Pe= 1158, 1202 and 1287. As the flow rate is closer to each other aproximate same phase lag is observed and that remains constant at various flow rate. It deccreases marginally with increase of flow rate.

5.4 FRONT SPEED AND FRONT SPREAD

The front speed and front spread are used to measure the diffusive and advective transport property in porous medium. The front speed is measured for 0.5 degree temperature rise between two locations. The non dimensional value is calculated by equation

$$\text{Front speed} = \frac{\Delta Z}{Pe\,\Delta t}$$

Where Pe is Peclet number and Δz is the distance between locations for the rise of 0.5temperature in Δt time.

The front speed is calculated at various locations and values are shown in Figure 5.09 (a) for hot and cold phase. The front speed is evaluated at two different *Pe* and shown in Figure 5.10(a).

The phenomenon of front spread arises from flow of fluid, when it is moving in pores of porous media. It is due to spreading of fluid particals in both the directions longitudenal and transvrse for dispersion. As the fluctuation of vlocity and temperature in longitudenal direction is high, the value of pulse speed is higher. The heat flow in transverse direction is low, therefore the front spread is also low but significant. For the higher dispersion and heat loss higher is the front spread. The front spread at particular location indicates the role of difussion in heat energy transfer. It is measured for the fluid temperature to rise from 0.25 to 0.75 at the location. The non dimensional value of front spread is calculated by the equation

Front Spread= (Δt) Pe

Where *Pe* is Peclet Number and Δt is the time to rise from 0.25 to 0.75. The front spread is calculated at various locations and values are shown in Figure 5.9 (b) for hot and cold phases.

The front spread is function of *Pe*, higher the value of *Pe*, the higher is the front spread. Front spread is experimentally examined at two different *Pe*= 1287 & 1202 and expressed graphically in Figure 5.10 (b).

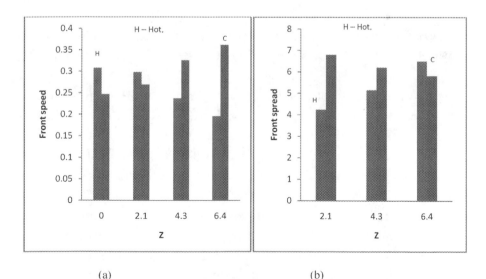

(a) (b)

***Figure** 5.9:* Value of (a) front speed (b) front spread in hot and cold phase at various locations in steel water bed d_p = 4.55 mm at *Pe= 1287& ω = 0.034 rad/s*

The Figure 5.9 shows the variation of front speed and front spread

The bar chart shows that front speed I hot phase is high at Z= 0 and decreases with the distance. Its value At Z= 0 is 0.308 and decreases to 0.196 at Z=8.6. In cold phase it increases from 0.24 to 0.36 frm Z= 0 to Z= 8.6. The value for the cold phase is maximum at Z= 8.6. Front spread is minimum at Z= 0 of value 4.02 and increases to 6.02 at locationZ= 8.6 in hot phase. The results are in the reverse order during the cold phase as per the direction of water.

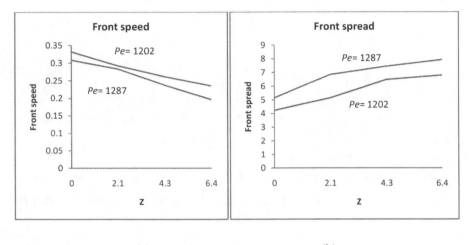

(a)   (b)

Figure *5.10:* Variation of (a) front speed (b) front spread with locations in steel water bed d_p = 4.55 mm at *Pe = 1202 & 1287 &* ω= *0.034 rad/s*

At *Pe* =1287 the front speed decreases with the locations and decrease of the front speed is linear from the hot domain to cold domain. It shows that energy transported by thermocouples near hot domain is more than the thermocouples near the cold domain. At *Pe* =1202 the variation of front speed with locations is also linear. At the thermocouples near hot inflow the value of front speed is 0.33 and reduces linearly to 0.235 at last thermocouples nearcold domain. The graph shows that heat absobed by thermocouples near hot domain is more as compared to heat absorbed by thermocouples near cold domain. Front speed is also higher at hot domain and decrease with downstream. Also with the decrease in *Pe* the front speed increases. It is obseved that front speed for hot phase is higher in first two locations and lower in last two locations as the hot fluid enters iat first thermouple.

The Figure 5.10(b) shows the variation of pulse spread with distance at Pe = 1287. Front spread at Z = 0 is 5.1 and rises to7.9 at location Z = 6.4. The front spread rises from hot domain to down stream. As the fluid flows with distance heat dispersion increases in longitudenal and transverse direction. At Pe =1202 the value of front spread at location Z = 0 is 4.40 and rises to 6.60 at location Z= 6.4. The spread rises to same rate for both Pe. The spread at Pe = 1287 is high and increases with Pe but slope of rise is same. The dispersion at high Pe number is more in longitudenal and transverse direction. The value of spread for cold phase is higher than the hot phase and increases from cold domain to hot domain.

The Figure 5.10(b) shows the variation of pulse spread with distance at Pe = 1287. Front spread at Z = 0 is 5.1 and rises to7.9 at location Z = 6.4. The front spread rises from hot domain to down stream. As the fluid flows with distance heat dispersion increases in longitudenal and transverse direction. At Pe =1202 the value of front spread at location Z = 0 is 4.40 and rises to 6.60 at location Z= 6.4. The spread rises to same rate for both Pe. The spread at Pe = 1287 is high and increases with Pe but slope of rise is same. The dispersion at high Pe number is more in longitudenal and transverse direction. The value of spread for cold phase is higher than the hot phase and increases from cold domain to hot domain.

5.5 THERMAL NON EQUILIBRIUM

When the hot/cold fluid flows through porous media in oscillating mode, the significant temperature difference exist between solid and fluid phase which is far away from thermal equilibrium and thermal non equilibrium exist between solid and liquid phase. In the initial stage of hot phase there is sharp rise in temperature called transiet state. The maximum energy exchange takes place between solid and liquid. In the steady state energy transfer between solid and liquid is minimum and temperature of solid/liquid does not vary. Thermal non equilibrium between solid and liquid is determined by measuring interphase temperature between solid and liquid. Thermal non equilibrium varies for hot and liquid phase. The temperature in hot phase keeps fluctuating between solid and liquid phase. The interphase temperature of solid and liquid phase is measured experimentally at Pe = 1287 at Z = 4.3 location. The maximum and minimum value of thermal non equilibrium is shown in Table

5.3. The variation of thermal non equilibrium with time at *Pe* = 1287 is shown in Figure 5.11.

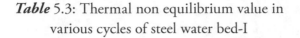

Table 5.3: Thermal non equilibrium value in
various cycles of steel water bed-I

Cycle	1	2	3
Maximum value of thermal non equilibrium	0.023	0.021	0.019
Minimum value of thermal non equilibrium	-0.018	-0.019	-0.021

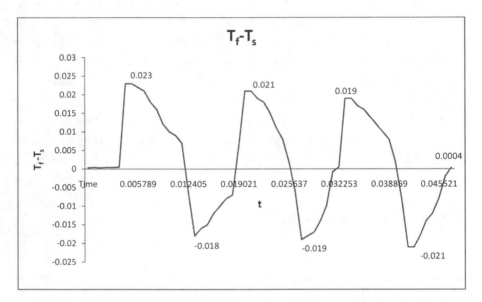

Figure *5.11:* Variation of thermal non equilibrium with time in steel
water bed d_p = 4.55mm at *Pe =1287 & ω= 0.034 rad/sec.*

As the temperature fluctuate in hot and cold phase, the temperature of solid and liquid phase keep changing. In hot phase, hot fluid enters at hot domain temperature of solid phase is slightly less than the cold phase. In cold phase cold fluid enters at opposite end, temperature of solid phase is slightly more than liquid phase. Thermal equilibrium in the hot phase is greater than cold phase at initialy phase and amplitude at initial cycle is 0.041. The maximum value of thermal equilibrium in hot phase is 0.024 and minimum value in cold phase is 0.021. Mamimum value of thermal equilibrium decreases in successive cycles. The rate of heat energy storage is higher at initial phase and the heat energy stored in hot phase is more than the heat retrival in cold phase.

5.6 HEAT ENERGY STORAGE AND RETRIEVAL

The sudy of heat transfer from an object placed in oscillating flow is attracting much research intrest due to its value for development and improvement in heat generators. As per the heat transfer characterstics the investgation is very exiquous. Studies in a similar geometry can be found in thermoascoustic field, but the oscillating flow conditions in such experimental investigations are very much difficult from the regenerators. Due to heat energy exchanged between different phases the porous media have application in major filed like oil exacters.

The energy storage system in the poros media stores the available energy in the solid phase and release the heat energy when the supply of energy is less. The poros media acts as thermal capacitor, absorbing the heat energy when exposed to hot fluid and releasing to heat energy when exposed to cold fluid. The ideal poros media shuold have high heat capacity to store heat energy offer minimum resistance for the fluid flow. The storage and retrieval of heat energy form solid material can be obtained by periodical flowing of hot and cold fluid. When the direction of hot and cold fluid is opposite, it is called the oscillating flow. The oscillating flow has two phases hot and cold. In hot phase hot fluid enters the bed at hot domain and exchange the heat energy to solid phase and flows out to other end. In cold phase, the cold fluid enters from the other end called cold domain, the cold fuild retrieves the stored energy from the solid material and flow out from the hot domain end. Thermal non equilibrium plays the key rule in heat energy exchange between the solid and liquid materials. The temparture differential are set up between solid and liquid in both phases. In hot phase the temparture of fluid phase is higher than cold phase and energy flows from the fluid to the solid phase. In cold phase the solid phase temparture higher than fluid temparture and heat energy flows from solid to the fuild. The heat capacity of poros media will be high when the effective surface area is large. The effective surface area is given by the equation.

$$A_{lf} = \frac{6(1-\varepsilon)}{d_p}$$

Where ϵ is porosity of bed and for steel bed I its value is 0.435, d_p is the diameter of spherical beads, its value is 4.55 mm. The effective surface value for the steel water bed is 745 m²/m³ of volume of bed which is quite large for immediate heat storage and retrival. To enchance the heat energy between solid and liquid phase the flow of fluid through the tortous in solid phase provide intense mixing between solid and liquid phase. The thermal performance of poros medium for energy storage in osscilliatry flow in steel water bed is discussed in this chapter as the thermal performance depends upon the thermal properties but the other properties such as flow rate, frequency of oscillation, effective surface area, particle size, no. of cycles, thermal non equilibrium have a significant role of thermal performance. The glass and plastic have properties close to water and steel properties are quite diffirent for thermal behaiour. The energy storage system is shown in Figure 5.12.

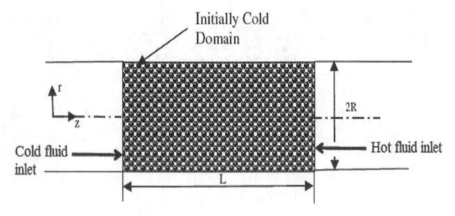

Figure 5.12: Energy storage system

In the energy storage system, the spherical steel beads are closely packed inside the insulated plastic tube of rodes. R= 42 mm. The length of plastic tube is L= 660 mm used for energy storage and rerival. The flow in poros bed is fully saturated at the constant head of 1100 mm. The porous bed is maintained at initailly non dimensial zero temparture. The velocity of fluid through the bed is senusoidal changing its direction after each phase. The variation of tempature with time is like sine wave form as shown in frequency response.

The hot phase is connsidered as positive half in which the hot fluid enters the bed through hot domain end and temparture of bed rises. The rise of temparture is sharp near the hot domain and decrease with down stream. The value of temparture near at Z= 0 is nearly unity and decrease with distance approaches to zero near at Z= L. The cold phase is considered as negative phase in which the cold water enter the cold domain through the opposite end. The temparture in the cold phase decends and approaches to zero at the end of phase. In the hot phase the temparture at a location rises due to storage of energy and decreases due to reterival of energy. During the unsteady state the maximum value of temperature changes from cycle to cycle, but in the study state the no change occurs in successive cycle. These profile are used to determine the parameter used for calculating the energy storage and energy reterival. The storage energy can be calculated by the rises in temparture of solid and fluid in the bed. The integration of solid and fluid phase temparture over a length of bed for particular point of time gives energy level. The storage energy for the particular time period can be calculate by the difference of energy level between the start and end of phase. The heat energy stored is calculated by equations.

$$E_{stored} = \int_{0}^{t_p/2} (\rho c_p)_f\, u\, sin(\omega t)\pi R^2 \left(T_{hot} - T_{cold}\right)_{z=0} dt$$
$$- \int_{0}^{t_p/2} (\rho c_p)_f\, u\, sin(\omega t)\pi R^2 \left(T - T_{cold}\right)_{z=L} dt$$

Where T is the temperature of hot fluid leaving the bed at cold end.

Similarly The heat energy retrived during cold phase is calculated by equation:

$$E_{retrieved} = \int_{t_p/2}^{t_p} (\rho c_p)_f\, u\, sin(\omega t)\pi R^2 \left(T - T_{cold}\right)_{z=0} dt$$
$$- \int_{t_p/2}^{t_p} (\rho c_p)_f\, u\, sin(\omega t)\pi R^2 \left(T_{cold} - T_{cold}\right)_{z=L} dt$$

Where T is the temperature of cold fluid leaving the bed at hot end.

The amount of heat energy stored and retrived at Pe= 1287& 1158 is listed in Table 5.4 & 5.5 and shown in Figure 5.13 & 5.14 respectively.

Table 5.4: Energy stored and retrived in cycle at *Pe = 1158 & ω=0.034 rad/s*

Cycle No.	1	2	3	4
E_{stored} kJ	2.20	1.85	1.73	1.69
$E_{Retrived}$ kJ	1.90	1.74	1.62	1.59

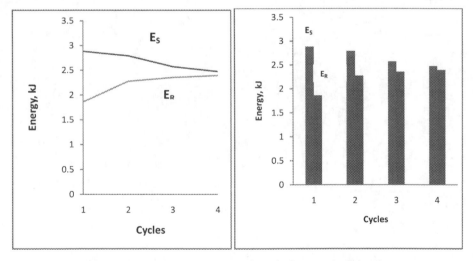

Figure *5.13:* Heat Energy stored and retrieved in steel water bed *d_p* = 4.55 mm at *Pe =1158 & ω=0.034 rad/s*

Table 5.5: Energy stored and retrived at Pe= 1287 *& ω=0.034 rad/s*

Cycles	1	2	3
E_{stored} kJ	2.40	2.35	2.25
$E_{Retrieved}$ kJ	2.06	2.14	2.20

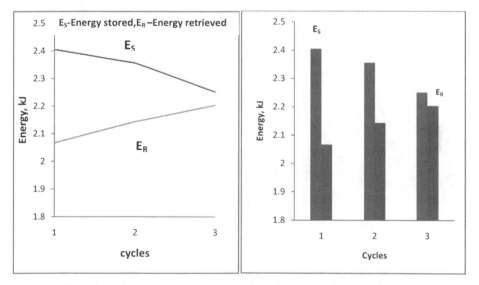

Figure 5.14: Heat Energy stored and retrieved in steel water
bed d_p = 4.55 mm at *Pe= 1287& ω=0.034 rad/s*

The amount heat energy stored and retrieved is calculated at two flow
rate *Pe* = 1287 and 1158 for number of cycles and shown in above figures. It is
observed that heat energy stored at initially cold domain is higher and decrease
with successive cycles. At Pe = 1287 heat energy stored at location Z= 2.1 is
2.45 kJ and decreases to 2.25 kJ in three cycles. The heat energy retrieved

during the first cycle is 2.06 kJ and increase to 2.23 kJ in three cycles. The heat energy stored decreases in successive cycles and heat energy increases in successive cycles. The value of heat energy stored and retrieved approaches to each after few cycles. The heat energy stored at Pe =1158 is also large at initial stage and decreases in successive cycles. But the amount of heat energy stored is less as compared Pe= 1287. The amount of heat energy stored and retrieved approaches to each other after six cycles and the amount of energy stored is approximately equal to amount of energy retrieved. The porous system is effective for retrieval of stored energy. The energy stored at high flow rate is large as compared to flow rate Pe = 1158.

5.7 EXPERIMENT VALIDATION

To certify the result obtained in various experiments, it is necessary to compare the results with standard data. The data obtained for the various thermal parameters like front amplitude, front spread are compared with the standard data and shown in figures.

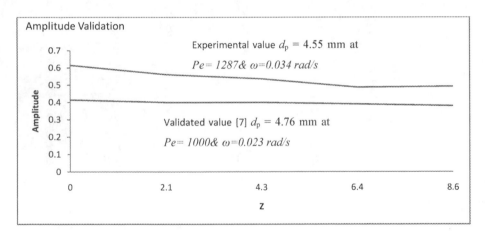

Figure 5.15: Comparision of expermental data of amplitude in steel water bed d_p = 4.55 mm at Pe= *1287&* ω=*0.034 rad/s* with standard data

The Figure 5.15 shows the comparision ofexperimental with standard data in section 9.2.2 of [7]. As the value of amplitude increases with increses of Pe and frequency of oscilation as per [7]. The similar resuts are obtained with the values very close tostandard results as shown in figure, which ensures the validation of the experiments.

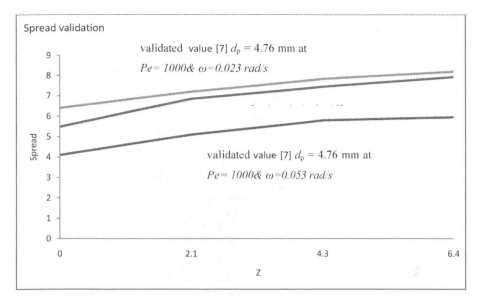

Figure 5.16: Comparision of expermental data of front spread in steel water bed d_p = 4.55 mm at *Pe= 1287& ω=0.034 rad/s* with validated data

The experimental data obtained for front spread in hot phase are compared with standard data of section 9.2.3 of [7] in Figure 5.16. As the experiment is performed with the similar boundary conditions the results showsthe similar trends. The experimental values at *Pe* = 1287 for size d_p = 4.55 in steel water bed at frequency value 0.034 rad/s lies between the frequency value of 0.023 rad/s and0.053 rad/s for size d_p = 4.76 mm in steel water bed at *Pe* = 1000. The front spread increases with distance in three graphs. The experimental values obtained are similar to standard results, hence results are satisfactory.

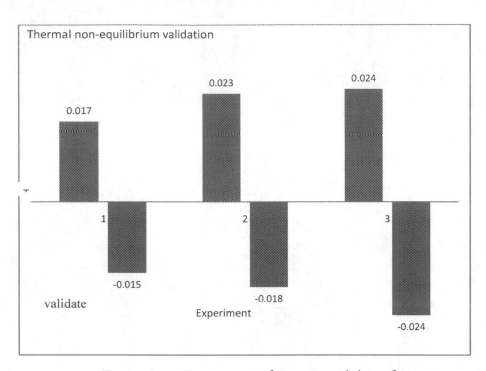

Figure 5.17: Comparision of expermental data of
thermal non-equilibrium in steel water bed d_p = 4.55 mm
at *Pe= 1287& ω=0.034 rad/s* with validated data

The Figure 5.17 shows the comparison of maximum and minimum value
of thermal non-equilibrium obtained in experiment with the standard value.
The maximum value 0.023 and minimum value -0.018 obtained in steel water
bed experiment size d_p = 4.55 mm at *Pe*= 1287& ω=0.034 rad/s at location Z=
4.3 lies between the values of frequencies 0.023 rad/s and 0.053rad/s in steel
water bed d_p = 4.76 mm at *Pe*= 1000 at location 4.9 mentioned in section 9.4
of [7]. Hence the experiments shows the acurate results.

5.8 CLOSURE

The frequency response of steel water bed I was dicussed in this chapter.
The material used in the porous bed was spherical steel balls of diameter
4.55 mm. The beads were closely packed in the bed and fully saturated flow
was maintained at constant head in oscillatory flow. By considering thermal
properties of steel, experiment were carried out at three flow rate *Pe* = 1158,

1202 & 1287. The variation of temperature with time were represented graphically for hot and cold phases. The variation of the temperature with location at different time were shown graphycally. The front amplitude and phase lag is discussed at three flow rates. The front amplitude is higher near the hot domain and decreases with the distance. The amplitude of location near the cold domain is low and increases with distance at margin rate. The front speed and spread are calculated for hot and cold phase. The front speed is found to be decreasing with the distance. The front spread is incresing with the distance. The front speed and front spread were different at different flow rate. It is concluded that front spread is more at higher flow rate. The increased front spread had enhanced the heat storage capacity. Thermal non equilibrium is discussed at three flow rate. The value for thermal non equilibrium is highewr for hot phase and decreases with the distance. The amount of heat energy stored and retrieved were calculated for hot and cold phases in three flow rate. The amount of heat energy stored at hot domain is large as compared to energy retrieved but aproaches each other in steady state. The amount of heat energy stored at higher Pe =1287 is large as compared to lower flow rate. The parameters like amplitude, spread and thermal non-equilibrium are compared with the results of [7] and results were found to be satisfactory.

CHAPTER 6

FREQUENCY RESPONSE OF GLASS WATER BED

6.1 INTRODUCTION

In chemical industries the glass material is used in many operations and it is desirable to analysis the thermal behavior of glass material at various boundary conditions. The thermal response of glass water bed for oscillating boundary conditions is discussed in this chapter and analyzed in terms of measurable factors such as front amplitude, front spread, front speed and phase lag. Besides the amount of heat energy stored during the hot phase and amount of energy retrieved during the cold phase is determined at various flow rates. Thermal non-equilibrium between the solid and the fluid phases is also determined.

In the previous chapter, the frequency response of steel water bed having particle diameter (d_P) of 4.55 mm was discussed. The thermo-physical properties of glass, as mentioned in Table 6.1, are distinct as compared to those of steel, as shown in Table 4.1; hence the thermal response is expected to be different.

Table 6.1: Thermal physical properties of glass

Thermal conductivity, k [W(mK)$^{-1}$]	Thermal storage capacity, ρc_P [kJm^{-3}K^{-1}]	Thermal diffusivity, α [m^{2}s^{-1}]
1.69	1869	0.583x10^{-6}

A closely packed spherical beads of d_P = 6.5 mm in an insulated PVC pipe with water flowing through constitutes the glass-water porous bed. The thermo-physical properties of bed are shown in Table 6.2.

Thermal capacity ratio $\beta = \dfrac{(\rho c_p)_f}{(\rho c_p)_s}$	Thermal conductivity ratio $\lambda = \dfrac{(k)_f}{(k)_s}$	Particle diameter, dp (mm)	Tube to particle diameter D/d_p	Porosity ϵ	Affective Surface area m^2/ m^3
2.2	0.55	6.5	12.92	0.380	572.3

Glass has a lower thermal conductivity as compared to that of steel but has a higher value of thermal storage per unit bed weight. A large value of tube to particle diameter ratio of 12.92 ensures a near flat velocity profile [7]. The affective surface area of bed is 572.3m^2/m^3, ensures sufficient interface heat transfer between the solid and the fluid phases. The bed has 660 mm suitable length for frequency response and suitable lengths at its two ends are kept to allow for flow development.

The hot and the cold water flows alternately through the opposite ends of the porous bed. The respective flow is for a time of 90 seconds each. Hence the total time period (t_p) is 180 seconds. When the hot water flows through the porous bed, called hot phase, the temperature at any location in the bed rises. It falls with the flow of cold water through opposite end, called cold phase. The hot and the cold phases constitute one thermal cycle. During the hot phase, the temperature in the bed rise and thermal energy is stored in it. During the cold phase, the temperature falls and the energy are retrieved. The respective rise and fall in temperature constitutes a cyclic variation as shown in the next section.

6.2 FREQUENCY RESPONSE AND CYCLIC TEMPERATURE PROFILES

The cyclic temperature profiles of glass water bed are discussed in this section. The porous bed is initially maintained at a zero temperature and with hot water flow its temperature rises to higher value. During the flow of cold water through the cold end the temperature at a location of bed falls to lower value which is more than zero. In the second cycle as the hot water flows through the hot end the temperature raises again but to a higher value than that of the previous cycle. It again falls with the flow of cold water. When the temperature at any instant of a cycle changes from one cycle to another, it is called the unsteady state. During the steady state, there is no temperatures variation from one cycle to another.

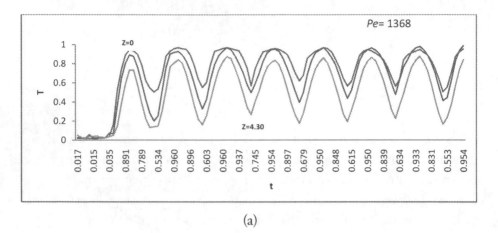

(a)

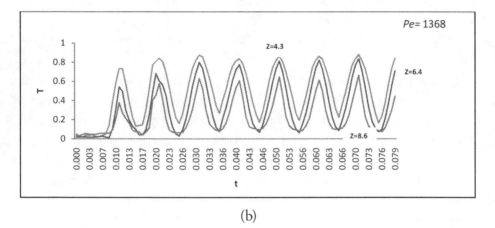

(b)

Figure 6.1: Variation of temperature with time in glass water bed at
(a) Z= 0, 2.1& 4.3 (b) *Z = 4.3, 6.4 & 8.6,*
d_p = 6.5 mm, *Pe =1368 & ω= 0.0349 rad/s*

Figure 6.1 shows variation of temperature with time at various locations in glass water bed at *Pe* =1368 *and* t_p = 180 second; thereby ω= *0.0349 rad/s.* Figure 6.1 (a) shows the variation of temperature at locations Z = 0, 2.1 & 4.3 and Figure 6.1 (b) shows the variation at locations *Z* = 4.3, 6.4 & 8.6. The locations Z = 0 and 8.6 are respectively called as the hot and the cold ends. The temperature at Z= 0 during the first hot phase rises to 0.91and subsequently falls to a value of 0.50. At location Z = 2.1 the temperature rises to a value 0.89, which is less as compared to that at location Z= 0, and subsequently falls to value of 0.21. Similarly the corresponding values at locations Z = 4.3 are 0.73 and 0.14. Hence highest and lowest temperature falls with distance from the hot end. The steady state is reached after 3-4 cycles. Figure 6.1(b) shows the variation of temperature towards the cold end. At location Z= 6.4 the temperature rise to 0.54, which is less than temperatures near the hot end. It falls to a minimum value of 0.04. At location Z = 8.6 the temperature rises to lowest value of 0.37 due to most of the heat is absorbed by previous locations and falls to 0.04. The value of maximum temperature at Z= 0 (hot domain) is quite high as compared to value at Z= 8.6, which indicates that most of the energy is stored at hot domain. Similarly the minimum temperature is at location Z= 8.6 (cold domain).

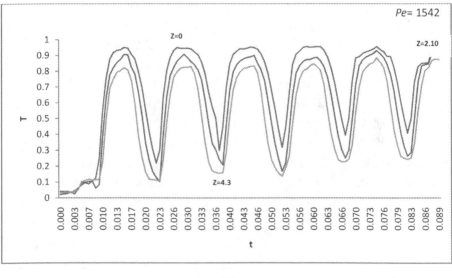

(a)

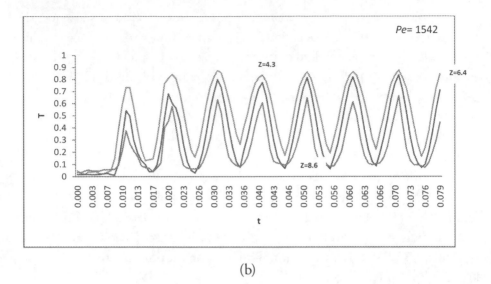

(b)

Figure *6.2:* Variation of temperature with time in glass
water bed at (a) *Z= 0, 2.1 & 4.3 (b) Z= 4.3, 6.4 & 8.6,*
*d*ₚ *= 6.5 mm, Pe = 1542 & ω = 0.0349 rad/s*

The figure 6.2 shows the variation of temperature at *Pe* = 1542 at various locations. In Figure 6.2 (a) at hot domain the temperature at Z = 0 location rises to value of 0.93 which is higher than *Pe* =1368 of value 0.91 at same location and falls to value of 0.30. At location Z= 2.1temperature rises to 0.90 which is also higher and falls to 0.16. In steady state the temperature at Z= 0 fluctuate between 0.94 & 0.40 and between 0.89 & 0.38 at Z= 2.1. The Figure 6.2 (b) shows the similar trends as in the previous case but the minimum temperature at Z = 6.4 remain at lower to value of 0.06 for short time period from the comparison of temperature profiles at *Pe* = 1368. At location Z = 8.6 the temperature rises to value of 0.37 and further rises to 0.60 in the steady state. The fall of temperature at location Z = 8.6 is at high rate and decreases to lower value 0.065 in the steady state. The sharp rise and fall of temperature indicates the low thermal conductivity of porous media. It is observed that at Z = 0 & 2.1 the maximum value remains for small period of time because the hot water enters at hot domain. Similarly at Z= 8.6 & 6.4 the lowest value remains for short while due to entrance of cold water at cold domain. The maximum temperature at all the locations increases in proceeding cycles and reaches to constant value in steady state.

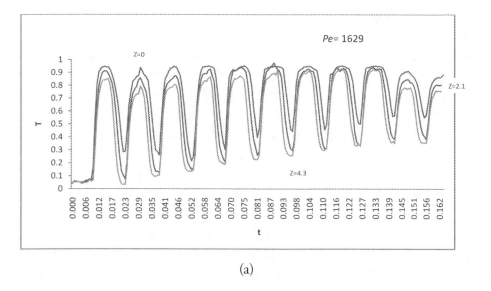

(a)

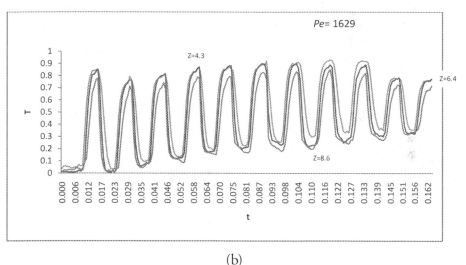

(b)

Figure 6.3: Variation of temperature with time in glass water bed at
(a) *Z= 0, 2.1 &4.3 (b) Z= 4.3, 6.4 & 8.6,*
d_p = 6.5 mm, Pe =1629 & ω= 0.0349 rad/s

The cyclic temperature response at *Pe*= 1629 is shown in Figure 6.3 for all the five locations.

The temperature profiles at flow rate *Pe* =1629 is compared with the profiles at *Pe* = 1542, the value of maximum temperature is high at all the locations. The Figure 6.3 (a) shows that at Z= 0 the value of temperature rises to 0.94 which is higher than that of 0.93 at *Pe= 1542* and falls to lower value of 0.026. The temperature at Z= 2.1 rises to value of 0.90 and further increases to 0.92 value after four cycle and temperature fluctuate between the value 0.92 and 0.39 in the steady state. The value obtained in steel water bed I at *Pe= 1287* and Z= 2.1 is 0.71 which is quite low as compared to glass water bed at same location due to the low thermal capacity of glass water bed. It is observed that value of maximum temperature is high at high flow rate at the same locations. Also the value of maximum temperature is high for glass material as compared to steel material. The Figure 6.3 (b) shows the similar trends at cold end. At location Z = 6.4 the temperature rises to the value of 0.80 and subsequently falls to value of 0.02 which is lowest. At Z = 8.6 the temperature rises to value of 0.76 and falls to minimum value of 0.016. The fall of temperature to low value is due to high flow rate. The value of maximum temperature approaches to constant value at all the locations as the steady state is established. The value of minimum temperature also increases with the cycles at high flow rate.

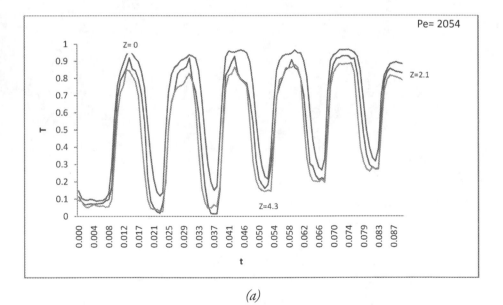

(a)

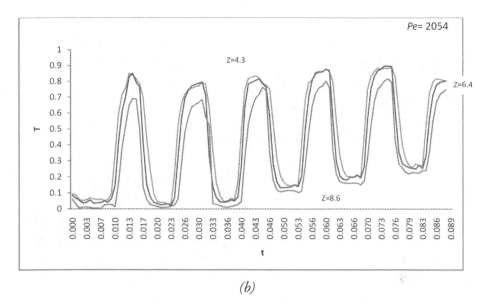

(b)

Figure 6.4: Variation of temperature with time in glass water bed at
(a) *Z= 0, 2.1 & 4.3 (b) Z= 4.3, 6.4 & 8.6,*
d$_\mathrm{p}$ = 6.5 mm, *Pe =2054 &* ω*= 0.0349 rad/s*

Figure 6.4 shows variation of temperature with time at various locations in glass water bed at high flow rate *Pe =2054 and t*$_p$ = 180 second; thereby ω= *0.0349 rad/s.* Figure 6.4 (a) shows the variation of temperature at locations Z = 0, 2.1 & 4.3 In Figure 6.4 (a) the temperature rises to maximum value of 0.96 at location Z= 0 which is higher than at *Pe=* 1629 value 0.94 at same location and falls to 0.11. In steel water bed the maximum value at *Pe =* 1287, Z= 0 is 0.82 which is quite low as compared glass water bed. Also the rise of temperature at other locations is high. At location Z= 2.1 the value of temperature rises to 0.92, also the value at adjacent location Z= 4.3 is 0.84. At higher flow rate at locations Z= 0, 2.1 & 4.3 the rise of temperatures are close to each other as large amount of water flows in same time period. Similarly the decrease of temperature is sharp and touches the lowest value as shown at Z= 2.1 to 0.04 value. The Figure 6.4 shows that the minimum temperature at Z= 8.6 is 0.02 and remains lower for small period of time for three cycles. The same trend is obtained at location Z= 6.4 and the minimum value remains low at 0.03. The minimum temperature increases after four cycles. It is concluded that he value of maximum temperature increases with the increase in flow rate at all the locations. Also the slope of rise and fall at high flow rate is high. The rise of temperature is high in glass water bed as compared to steel water bed discussed in Chapter 5. The experimental result obtained in this section are compared with the result of [7] chapter 8 section 8.5.2. The results obtained are at satisfactory level and similar trends are obtained.

6.2.1 Maximum and Minimum Temperature

The experiments are carried out at different flow rate and input hot water temperature. The various results are obtained by changing the flow rate and inlet hot water temperature. The temperature profile will be drawn at all the thermocouples. As the hot water enters at hot domain the temperature rises in bed and falls in the cold phase. The rise of temperature at various locations to maximum value temperature and fall to lower value in hot and cold phase is shown Figure 6.5 & 6.6.

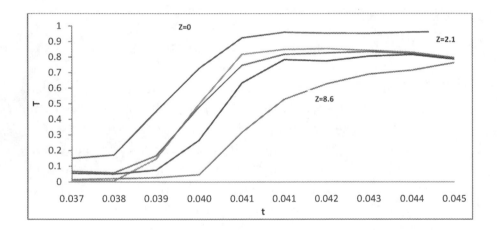

***Figure** 6.5*: Temperature rise at various locations in
hot phase at *Pe =2054, time period= 0.008*

It is observed that rise of temperature is very smooth at all locations. The maximum rise of temperature is at hot domain. The gap of temperature between the locations is uniform. The temperature at Z= 0 remains at highest value as the hot water enters at hot domain. The temperature at Z= 6.4 is at less value due to water dissipated the heat at previous locations. At Z= 8.6 the value remains the minimum being located at end. The temperature closes to each other at end of 120 seconds (0.008) and reaches to maximum value for all locations.

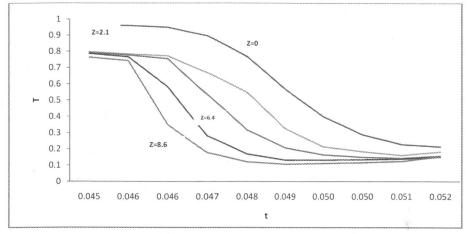

Figure *6.6*: Temperature fall at various locations in cold phase at *Pe =2054, time period= 0.008*

The fall of temperature is in the same trend as the temperature rise in case of hot phase. The temperature decreases smoothly and with uniform gap of temperature. The temperature decreases sharply at the location Z= 8.6 as the cold water enters at cold domain and flows in opposite direction. The temperature decreases slowly at the location Z= 0 as located at the hot end. The temperature approaches to lowest value at the end of cold phase. The value of temperatures at all locations closes to single value as maximum heat is dissipated. The maximum and minimum value in the hot and the cold phase reaches in time 0.004 which is less as compared to steel water bed shown in section 5.3.2. The results obtained as shown in Figure 6.5 & 6.6 are compared with value in Chapter 6 of [7] and the results found satisfactory.

The value maximum temperature is not same at all the locations and changes with the passage of time. The peak value for the location near hot domain is higher and decreases with the downstream. The variation of the peak temperature at different locations for different time is shown in the Figure 6.7.

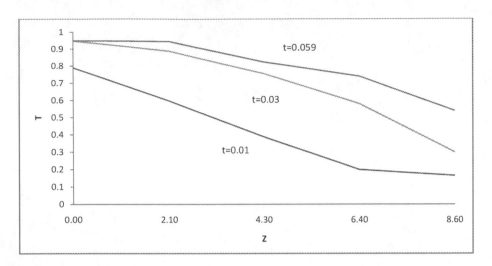

Figure *6.7:* Variation of peak temperature with locations in glass
water bed d_p = 6.5 mm at *Pe =1368 &* ω*= 0.0349 rad/s*

The peak value variations are shown for the different flow rate. It is observed that variation of peak at hot domain is higher and decreases with the locations. The peak value at time t = 0.01 at location Z= 0 is 8.1 and rises to 9.1 at time t = 0.059. The peak value decreases with the time. The value of temperature at two thermocouples is higher near the hot domain and decreases with downstream.

flows in opposite direction. The temperature decreases slowly at the location Z= 0 as located at the hot end. The temperature approaches to lowest value at the end of cold phase. The value of temperatures at all locations closes to single value as maximum heat is dissipated. The maximum and minimum value in the hot and the cold phase reaches in time 0.004 which is less as compared to steel water bed shown in section 5.3.2. The results obtained as shown in Figure 6.5 & 6.6 are compared with value in Chapter 6 of [7] and the results found satisfactory.

The value maximum temperature is not same at all the locations and changes with the passage of time. The peak value for the location near hot domain is higher and decreases with the downstream. The variation of the peak temperature at different locations for different time is shown in the Figure 6.7.

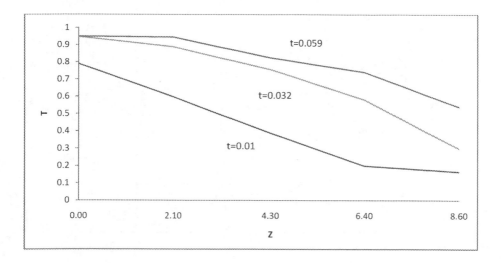

Figure *6.7:* Variation of peak temperature with locations in glass water bed d_p = 6.5 mm at *Pe =1368 &* ω= *0.0349 rad/s*

The peak value variations are shown for the different flow rate. It is observed that variation of peak at hot domain is higher and decreases with the locations. The peak value at time t = 0.01 at location Z= 0 is 8.1 and rises to 9.1 at time t = 0.059. The peak value decreases with the time. The value of temperature at two thermocouples is higher near the hot domain and decreases with downstream.

The value of minimum temperature is not same at all the locations. The minimum temperature varies with the locations at various times. The variation of valleys at different locations is shown in Figure 6.8.

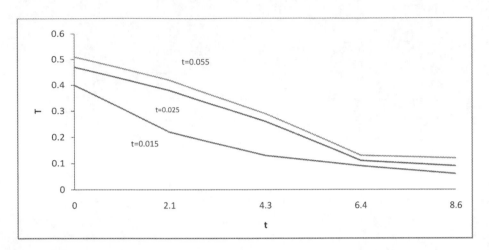

Figure 6.8: Variation of valley temperature with locations in glass water bed d_p = 6.5 mm at *Pe =1368 & ω= 0.0349 rad/s*

The valley temperature is observed at three instant of time. At time t= 0.015 the value of temperature at Z= 0 is 0.40 and reduces to 0.06 at location Z=8.6. At time t= 0.055 the minimum temperature at Z= 0 is 0.57 and reduces to 0.12 at Z= 8.6. The values at Z= 6.4 & 8.6 remains constant as the cold water enters at hot domain in the opposite direction. The minimum temperature at location Z=0 is high as the water retrieve the heat from solid material. The value of minimum temperature increases with the cycles. At The fluctuations of temperatures are high in three cycles and after 3-5 cycles, approaches to fixed value as the steady state is established.

6.3 AMPLITUDE AND PHASE LAG

The amplitude is the difference between the maximum and the minimum temperature at a location. It is observed from the frequency response that during first cycle the amplitude is high due to initially cold domain and decreases with time. The value of amplitude is calculated at three different time t_1= 0.029, t_2= 0.044 & t_3= 0.058 and shown at locations in bar chart in Figure 6.9. The variation of amplitude with time at various locations at *Pe =1629* & 1542 is shown in Figures 6.10 (a) and 6.11. The average time elapsed between successive peaks is known as phase lag. It represent time lag of occurrence of respective point on the curve. The phase lag the glass water bed is calculated at *Pe*= 1629 and shown in Figure 6.10 (b).

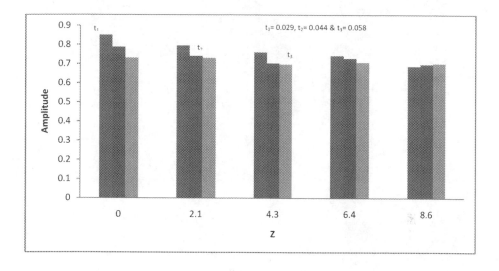

Figure 6.9: Variation of amplitude with locations in glass water bed
d_p = 6.5 mm at time t_1= 0.029, t_2= 0.044
& t_3= 0.058 at *Pe* =1629 & ω= 0.034 rad/s

The value front amplitude is calculated at three instant of time t_1= 0.029, t_2= 0.044 & t_3= 0.058, it is observed that difference of amplitude at Z= 0 is higher as compared to other locations except at Z= 8.6 in which the difference is negligible. The value of amplitude is decreasing with the locations at time t_1= 0.029 where as it is approximate uniform at time t_3= 0.058. It concludes that amplitudes fluctuate at initial stage and approaches to constant value as steady state reached.

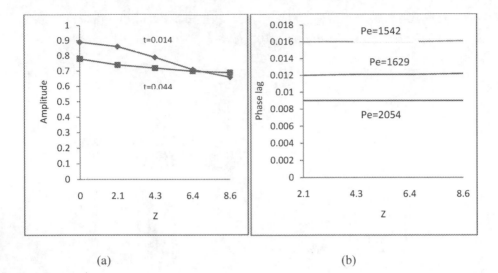

(a)   (b)

***Figure* 6.10**: Variation of (a) amplitude with locations at
Pe = *1629* (b) phase lag with locations in glass water
bed d_p = 6.5 mm & ω= *0.0349 rad/s*

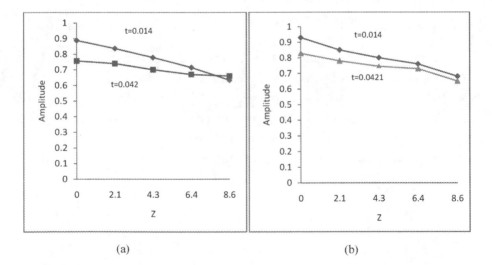

(a)   (b)

***Figure* 6.11:** Variation of amplitude with locations in glass water bed
d_p = 6.5 mm at *(a) Pe =1542 (b) Pe =2054*, ω= *0.0349 rad/s*

The Figure 6.10 shows that the amplitude at initial state at *Pe* = 1629 is higher
and decreases with time and locations. At location Z= 0 its value is 0.90 and reduces

to 0.64 at Z= 8.6. At time t= 0.44 the value at location Z= 0 is 0.8 and decreases to 0.69. But at cold domain the amplitude increases in cycles and after 3-5 cycles the amplitude at various location approaches each other. Similarly at *Pe* = 2054 the value of amplitude at location Z = 0 is 0.93 which is higher than other locations and higher than the value at *Pe* = 1629. Also the value of amplitude decreases with locations. The amplitude at Z = 8.6 location near the cold fluid entrance increases to 0.68. The amplitude at location near to hot water entrance is higher and decreases with the distance. The cold water enter at other end and lower the temperature at Z = 8.6 and amplitude increases with time. At *Pe*=1542 the value of amplitude at Z= 0 rises to 0.88 and at Z= 8.6 the value is 0.63. The same trends are obtained as in other flow rate. It concludes that in glass water bed the fluctuation of temperature is high and the value of amplitude is higher than steel water bed value 0.78 at Pe= 1287 as explained in Chapter 5. As the experiment is carried out at flow rate *Pe* = 2054, 1629 & 1542, the value of amplitude at *Pe* = 2054 is higher than the value of *Pe* = 1629. At high flow rate the amplitude increases.

It is observed from the Figure 6.10 (b) that the phase lag remains constant at various locations. The value of phase lag is low as compared to steel water bed I and decreases at high flow rate. The phase is analyzed at flow rate *Pe*= 2054, 1629 & 1542. As the flow rate is increased the phase lag is decreased. It is concluded that at constant frequency 0.0349 rad/s the amplitude decreases with distance but the phase lag remains constant for down streams.

6.4 VARIATION OF FRONT SPREAD AND FRONT SPEED

In glass water bed the experiments are carried out at three flow rate, *Pe* = 1542, 1629 and 2054 with different inlet hot water temperature. The frequency value 0.034 rad/s remains constant for all three types of experiments. The front speed and front spread is examined at these flow rates. Front speed is ratio of spatial distance to time for rise to 0.5. It measures the amount of heat absorbed. It is less than speed of water. It is calculated by equation 3.17 explained in Chapter 3.

The front speed is analyzed at *Pe* = 1542, 1629 and 2054. The Figure 6.13 (a) shows the front speed at Pe = 1542 & 2054. As the front spread is the change of temperature from 0.25 to 0.75 at a particular location. It is the thermal speed of water in transverse direction in which the heat travels in the glass water bed. As the heat energy is distributed to solid phase the front spread increases. The front spread at *Pe* = 1542, 2054 is shown in Figure 6.13 (b).

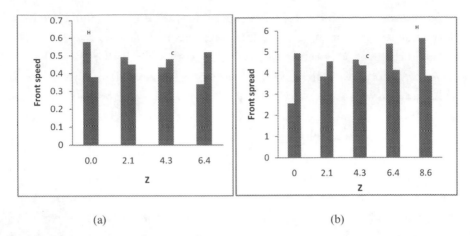

(a)   (b)

Figure *6.12:* Variation of (a) front speed and (b) front spread with locations in glass water bed d_p = 6.5 mm at *Pe = 1542 & ω= 0.0349 rad/s*

The Figure 6.12(a) shows that front speed decreases in hot phase and increases in the cold phase as cold water flows in opposite direction. The maximum value of front speed is higher for hot phase. Similarly the value of front spread increases in the hot phase and decreases in the cold phase. The value of front spread is highest for hot phase at Z= 8.6 where as it is lowest at Z= 0.

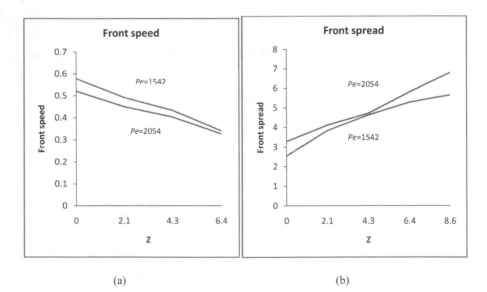

(a)   (b)

Figure *6.13:* Variation of (a) front speed and (b) front spread with distance in glass water bed d_p = 6.5 mm at *Pe = 1542 & 2054, ω= 0.0349 rad/s*

The Figure 6.13 (a) shows that the front speed at $Pe=$ 2054 is highest at $Z=0$ of and decreases with downstream, the value of front speed at location $Z = 0$ hot domain is 0.52 and reduces to the value of 0.32 at location $Z = 8.6$. The graphs shows that heat dissipation decreases with the increase in distance. At $Pe = 1542$ the value of front speed at $Z= 0$ is higher to value of 0.579 and decreases with distance to value of 0.34. The value of front speed is as compared to that of steel water bed I of value 0.31 at $Pe = 1287$ of same location. The front speed at lower Pe is higher. The decrease of front speed is at very low rate. It is observed from the graphs 6.13 (b) that the front spread increases in hot phase with downstream. At $Z = 0$ the temperature rises very fast and rate of temperature decreases is also high with distance. The value of spread at $Pe = 1542$ at location $Z= 0$ is 2.55 and increases to value of 5.65 at location $Z = 8.6$. It is lower as compared to steel waterbed I at $Pe= 1287$ of value 5.1. Also at higher Pe 2054 the value of front spread is 3.3 and rises to 6.8 at $Z= 8.6$. It gives the similar trends at higher flow rate. The front spread is largest at the $Z = 8.6$, because it takes the maximum time to reach temperature from 0.25 to 0.75. It concludes that front speed in glass water bed decreases with distance and increases at lower flow rate in hot phase. In cold phase the value of pulse speed is found to be increasing and front spread decreases as cold water enters at cold domain.

6.5 THERMAL NON EQUILIBRIUM

In the frequency response of oscillating flow in glass water bed temperature fluctuate between maximum and minimum value in hot and cold phase. In the cyclic unsteady state the temperature difference of hot fluid and solid material is large. In the hot phase fluid flowing in bed has higher temperature than solid materials and in cold phase fluid temperature is lower. In cyclic steady state the uniform temperature difference between the two phases fluctuates periodically on either side of the zero. Hence the thermal non equilibrium between fluid and solid phase fluctuate to either side of zero. In the hot phase when fluid temperature is higher than solid temperature is considered as positive thermal non equilibrium and in cold phase considered as negative. The value of positive and negative fluctuate in successive cycles of oscillating flow and there exist an amplitude between the maximum and minimum values. The thermal non equilibrium is analyzed at three Peclet numbers. The thermal non equilibrium at $Pe = 1542$ is presented at $Z= 2.1$ in Figure 6.14.

Table 6.3: Thermal non equilibrium value in various cycles of glass water bed *at Pe =1542, Z= 2.1 & ω= 0.0349 rad/s*

Cycle	1	2	3
Maximum value of thermal non equilibrium	0.0072	0.0058	0.0051
Minimum value of thermal non equilibrium	-0.0058	-0.0062	-0.0061

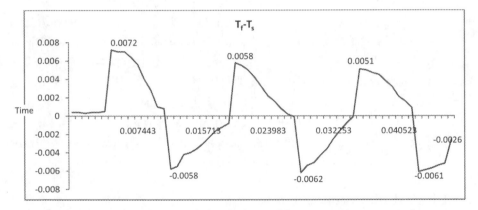

Figure 6.14: Variation of thermal equilibrium with time in glass water bed d_p = 6.5 mm at *Pe =1542 & ω= 0.0349 rad/s*

The thermal non equilibrium at location Z = 2.1 is shown in above graph. It is observed that the maximum value is recorded during hot phase and minimum value during cold phase. So the heat exchange during hot phase is higher than heat exchange during cold phase. The degree of thermal non equilibrium decreases in successive cycles. As the experiment is carried out at different flow rate, it is observed that the value of thermal non equilibrium increases with increase in flow rate. At higher *Pe* umber the value of thermal non equilibrium is higher. The amplitude of thermal non equilibrium is higher at hot domain Z= 0 and decreases with downstream as fluid enters hot domain at highest temperature T_h. The temperature of fluid decreases as it flows in the downstream. Heat absorbed near the hot domain is higher and decreases with the distance. Similarly the heat retrieved near the cold domain is lower and increases with distance. It is concluded that thermal non equilibrium near the hot domain is higher. The value of thermal non equilibrium increases with increases in flow rate. The amplitude of thermal non equilibrium decreases in successive cycles.

6.6 THERMAL STORAGE OF ENERGY

The heat storage and retrieval of energy in fixed glass solid masses are obtained by flow of hot and cold fluid in porous media. The porous medium energy storage system stores the excess available energy in solid phase and releases when the energy is on demand. The energy is stored as sensible heat. In this glass water bed the spherical glass balls of 6.5 mm diameter are used as solid material. The glass material has large effective surface area with value 572.3 m²/m³ of value of the bed. The flow of fluid through the voids has intense mixing of solid and fluid phases. The thermal conductivity of glass material is lower than steel and greater than water. The amount of energy stored is less in hot phase. The tube length of 660 mm and radius 42 mm is taken for storage and retrieval of heat energy. The spherical glass beads are closely packed in the tube and fully saturated flow at a constant head of 110 cm is maintained. The temperature profiles obtained in oscillatory flow at all thermocouples are in the wave form and has positive and negative phase. In the positive phase the hot water enters at hot domain and temperature rises to peak value. Heat energy is absorbed by solid materials in this phase. If the temperature of hot water entering hot domain is unity, the maximum rise of temperature is at Z = 0 and decreases with the distance. During the negative phase the cold water enters at opposite end and temperature decreases to lower value. If the fluid entering cold end is considered as with zero energy, the heat energy is gained by fluid in this phase. The heat energy is retrieved from the solid material. Amount of heat energy stored in positive phase and energy retrieved in negative phase is obtained by the energy equations discussed in previous chapter. Heat energy stored in positive phase is function of fluid temperature flowing out at exit end Z = L and heat energy retrieved is function of fluid temperature flowing out at domain Z = 0. Heat energy stored in first cycle is higher due to the initially cold bed and heat energy retrieved in first cycles is lower and increases in successive cycles. Heat energy stored and retrieved at two *Pe*= 1542 & 1629 is calculated for five cycles and shown in Figure 6.15 & 6.16.

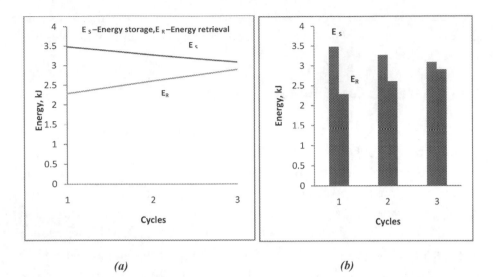

(a)   *(b)*

Figure *6.15:* Heat energy stored and retrieved in glass water bed at d_p = 6.5 mm *Pe =1542 & ω= 0.0349 rad/s* by (a) graph (b) bar chart

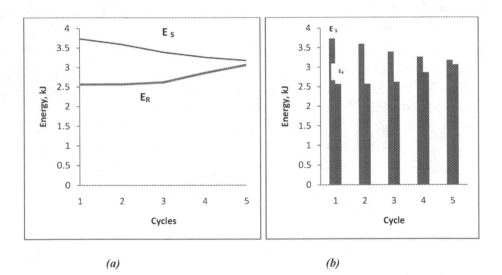

(a)   *(b)*

Figure *6.16:* Heat energy stored and retrieved in glass water bed d_p = 6.5 mm at *Pe =1629 & ω= 0.0349 rad/s* by (a) graph (b) bar chart

It is observed from the graph that at *Pe =1542* heat energy stored in first cycle is higher and decreases with the no of cycles. The heat energy retrieved in first cycle is low and increases in successive cycles. This is due to the initially cold domain. After four cycles the steady cyclic state approaches and amount of heat retrieved is close to the energy stored. At *Pe* = 1629 the amount of heat energy stored is higher in first cycle and amount of heat energy retrieved is lower. The value of heat energy stored decreases in successive cycles and energy retrieved increases in successive cycles. It is observed that amount of energy stored at high flow rate is higher. At *Pe* = 1629 amount of energy stored is 3.706 kJ which is higher than 3.557 kJ at *Pe* = 1542. The difference of energy stored and retrieval is large at higher flow rate and low at lower flow rate.

6.7 CLOSURE

The frequency response of glass water bed is analyzed at three flow rate *Pe* = 1368, 1542, 1629 & 2054. The glass beads of 6.5 mm diameter are used as solid material with oscillatory flow. Experiments are performed at different inlet hot water temperature. During the experiments sine wave profiles of temperature with respect to time are obtained. The temperature profile at all the locations are shown and compared. The temperature profiles are different than obtained in steel water bed I. The profile indicates sharp rise of temperature due to low conductivity of porous material. The profile at location Z = 0 and Z = 8.6 are different as the heat dissipates with flow. The variation maximum and minimum temperatures are shown at three different times at various locations. The rise of temperature in the hot and the cold phases are shown at all the locations. The front amplitude is analyzed at different instant of time. The amplitude at Z = 0 location were highest in the initial time and decreases with passage of time. Amplitude at Z = 8.6 location was low initially and approaches to Z = 0 amplitude after few cycles. While studying the phase lag, the uniform gap of temperature between two locations is obtained. The value of phase lag is lower than the steel water bed I and remains constant for all locations. The front spread is found to be increased at higher rate than steel water bed I. The thermal spread is found to be faster in glass water bed. The front speed is observed as decreasing but at very low rate. Value of front speed decreases at higher flow rate and it is higher than steel water bed I. Front spread is calculated for hot and cold phase. In cold phase the trends are observed opposite to hot phase as the cold water enters from cold domain. Thermal non equilibrium value for the glass water bed is very low and its value for hot phase is greater than cold phase. Amount of heat energy exchange is calculated at two flow rate. The heat energy exchange is higher at higher *Pe*. The value of heat energy stored and retrieved are different in the initial phase of experiment but approaches each other after few cycles. The parameters of thermal response obtained in glass water bed are compared with the results of [7] and found satisfactory.

CHAPTER 7

FREQUENCY RESPONSE OF STEEL WATER BED-II

7.1 INTRODUCTION

In the Chapters 5 the frequency response of steel water beds I having particle diameter d_p = 4.55 mm is discussed and in Chapter 6 the frequency response of glass water bed diameter d_p =6.5 is carried out. Though in these two chapters the solid phase is quite different but the particle size is not similar for effective comparison. Hence further study of frequency response of porous bed is necessitated. Easy availability of steel beads diameter d_p =6.5 mm ensures that the comparison is complete. The thermal physical properties of steel water bed are mentioned in Table 5.2 of Chapter 5, which shows the value of thermal conductivity ratio (λ) and Thermal capacity ratio (β). The thermal storage capacity ratio of water is higher than the steel but thermal conductivity ratio is marginally lower. The thermal diffusivity of steel 5.83×10^{-6} $m^2 s^{-1}$ is higher than that of water and glass. The physical properties of particle size d_p = 6.5 mm are mentioned in Table 6.1 of Chapter 6. It ensures that the effect of particle size on thermal response is effectively carried out. The flow rate and frequency is chosen similar to those in Chapter 5 & 6. In this chapter the frequency response graph, front amplitude, phase lag, front spread, front speed and thermal non-equilibrium is discussed. Besides the comparison with those of glass water bed size d_p = 6.5 mm and steel water bed d_p = 4.55 is also carried out. The amount of energy stored in steady and un steady state at various flow rates is presented graphically. The effect of heat loss is discussed.

7.2 FREQUENCY RESPONSE AND CYCLIC TEMPERATURE PROFILE

The frequency response of steel water bed II is discussed in this section. The cyclic temperature response at three flow rate for three locations is shown in each case. In oscillating flow the hot and the cold fluid flows through the bed alternately at opposite ends, the temperature of bed fluctuates between maximum and minimum value. The temperature profiles during the hot and cold phase are in the wave form but different from glass water bed and steel water bed I. The experiments are performed at the *Pe* = 1368, 1542 & 1888 and the temperature profiles are obtained. A frequency response has unsteady and cyclic steady state, the steady state reaches after 3-4 cycles in which temperature fluctuates between constant maximum and minimum temperature.

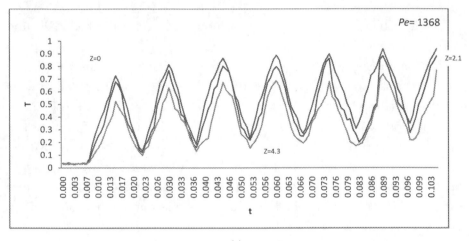

(a)

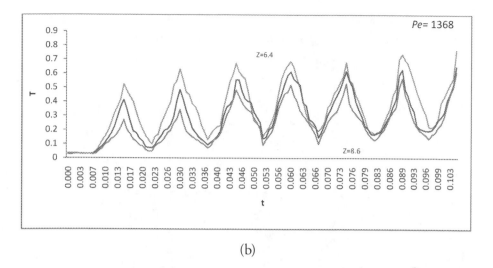

(b)

Figure 7.1 Variation of temperature with time in steel water bed
d_p =6.5 mm at (a) Z= 0, 2.1& 4.3 (b) Z = 4.3, 6.4
& 8.6, Pe =1368 & ω= 0.0349 rad/s

The Figure 7.1 shows the temperature profiles at Pe = 1368. In Figure 7.1(a) at Z = 0 and rise of temperature is faster as compared to other locations. The temperature rises to value of 0.72 and subsequently falls to value of 0.13 in first cycle. The maximum temperature is quite low as compared to glass water bed 0.92 and steel water bed 0.83 at same location as mentions in Chapter 5 & 6. The maximum value increases to high value 0.93 after four cycles as the steady state approaches. The minimum value also increases to 0.26 in the steady state and temperature fluctuates between these two values. At Z =2.1 the temperature rises to value of 0.67 and falls to value of 0.16 in the cold phase. At the location Z= 4.3 (midpoint) the temperature rises to 0.5 in first cycle and further increases to 0.64 value in the steady state. At the end of cold phase the minimum value falls to 0.093 and increases to 0.145. The fluctuation of temperature is at low levl as to location. The Figure 5.1 (b) at Z = 8.6 the value of temperature rises to 0.26 in the first cycle and increases to 0.56 after four cycles. The minimum value also increases marginally as the steady state approaches. The minimum value at locations Z= 8.6 & 6.4 remains minimum to 0.08 up to three cycles and increases marginally after four cycles. Due to high storage capacity and conductivity the rise of temperature is slow as compared to the steel water bed I and glass water bed. The slope of temperature rise is low at all the locations. The temperature at location is low as compared to steel water bed I so the large amount of energy is absorbed.

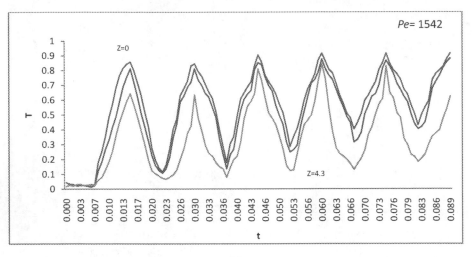

(a)

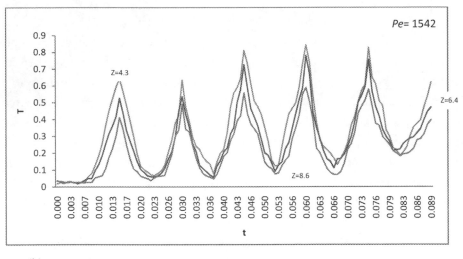

(b)

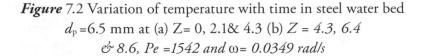

Figure 7.2 Variation of temperature with time in steel water bed d_p =6.5 mm at (a) Z= 0, 2.1& 4.3 (b) *Z* = *4.3, 6.4 & 8.6, Pe =1542 and* ω= *0.0349 rad/s*

The Figure 7.2 shows the temperature profile at Pe = 1542. The similar trends are observed as in previous experiment. In the first cycle the maximum temperature at all the locations is less as compared to successive cycles. In Figure 7.2 (a) the value of maximum temperature at Z = 0 near hot domain is 0.84, which is large as compared to Pe = 1368 value 0.68 but it is lower than glass water bed value 0.93 at the same location. The maximum temperature rise also increases as the steady state approaches. The maximum value at the adjacent location Z= 2.1 rises to 0.81 with the increase of flow and falls to value of 0.08 in the cold phase. Both the temperature profiles are close to each other. At Z=4.3 (midpoint) the maximum temperature rises to value of 0.67 and subsequently falls to value of 0.072. In Figure 7.2 (b) at Z= 8.6 the value of maximum temperature is minimum 0.41 and falls to lower value of 0.07 in the cold phase. At Z= 6.4 the temperature rises to maximum value of 0.57 and falls to value of 0.06 which is close to lower value of Z= 8.6. It is observed that at high flow rate the rise and the fall of temperature is sharp as compared to Pe = 1368 and temperature gap increases, which indicates that amount of heat energy transfer is increased. As the flow rate is increased the fluctuation amplitude is increased. The value of minimum temperature increases after four cycles. It is observed that with the increases of flow rate the rise of temperature increases but the rate of increase is less as compared to glass.

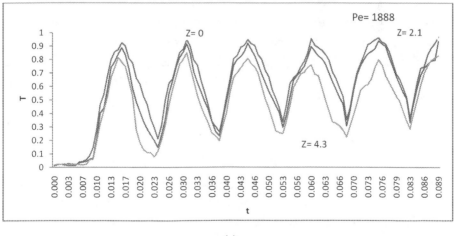

(a)

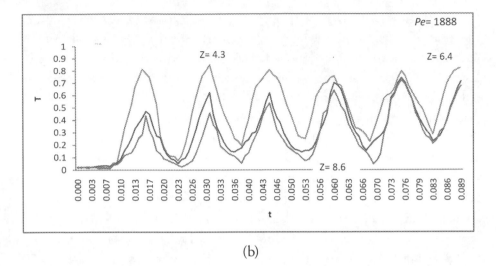

(b)

Figure 7.3: Variation of temperature with time in steel water bed
*d*_p =6.5 mm at (a) Z= 0, 2.1& 4.3 (b) *Z = 4.3, 6.4*
& 8.6, Pe =1888 and ω*= 0.0349 rad/s*

The Figure 7.3 shows the cyclic temperature profile at *Pe*= 1888. All the five locations temperature profiles are shown in Figure 7.3 (a) & (b). As the flow rate is increased to *Pe* = 1888 the rise of temperature to maximum value increases and same type of temperature profiles are obtained. The rise of temperature at Z= 0 is increased to value of 0.92 and further increases to 0.96 value after four locations. The minimum temperature value also increases with cycles from the value of 0.24 and increases to 0.47 in the steady state. At location Z= 4.3 (midpoint) the temperature rises to value of 0.81 and the minimum temperature value 0.08. At location the minimum temperature remains at low value 0.08 as cold water enters at high flow rate ar cold domain. The Figure 7.3 (b) at Z= 8.6 the temperature rises to 0.43 in first cycle which is higher as compared to Pe= 1368 & 1542. It increases to value of 0.72 in the steady state. The minimum temperature at location Z= 6.4 remains minimum at value 0.08 being nearer to cold domain. The temperature rises to high value at hot end and lower value at cold end. It is concluded that the rise of temperature in steel water bed II is at slow rate as compared to glass water bed and steel water bed I because large affective surface area and high capacity ratio. The rise of temperature increases with the increases in flow rate. The results obtained in this section are compared with the results of [7] and results are found satisfactory with similar trends.

7.2.1 Maximum and Minimum Temperature

As the hot water enter at hot domain and temperature rises to maximum values in the bed. The rise of temperature is in the wave from and the temperature in hot phase is different at various locations. The slope of rise of temperature is gentle and temperature rises to lower value. Similarly the cold fluid enters at opposite end and fall of temperature is different at various locations. The rise and fall of temperature at different locations is showing in Figures 7.4 & 7.5.

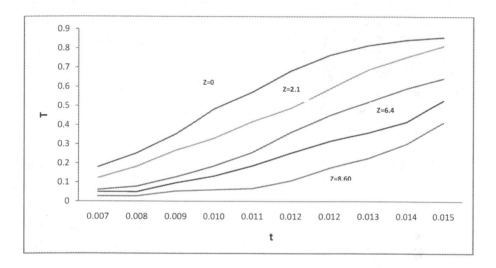

Figure 7.4: Rise of temperature with time in steel water bed
d_p = 6.5 mm in hot phase at *Pe = 1542 and time period= 0.008*

As the hot water enters at the hot domain, the temperature at Z= 0 is rises to maximum value of 0.85 but decreases with the distance. The hot fluid enters with maximum energy at Z= 0 and exchanges its energy with the solid material and temperature of the fluid decreases with the locations. The Temperature rises with gentle slope. There is uniform gap between temperatures of all locations. After the time t= 0.008 the temperature does close to each due slow rise of temperature as the porous material have high thermal capacity. There is no sharp rise in temperatures. The rise of temperature at Z= 8.6 location is minimum value of 0.41. The maximum temperature varies linearly with the locations.

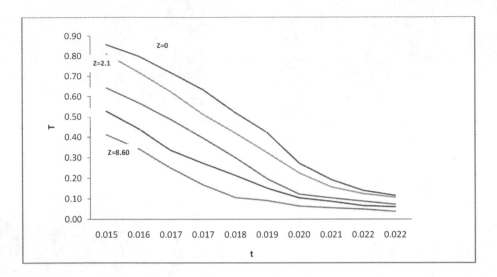

Figure 7.5: Temperature fall at various locations in cold phase in steel water bed d_p = 6.5 mm at *Pe =1542 and time period= 0.008*

In the cold phase the decrease of temperature at Z=8.6 goes to minimum value as compared to other locations. The similar trends are obtained as in case of hot phase. The temperature decreases smoothly at all locations. The temperature gap between the locations is approximately uniform. The temperature approaches to each other at the minimum value in the end of cold phase (0.008).

The variation of peak temperature is different at different locations. The value of peak temperature increases with the increase of flow rates. The peak value is analyzed at three instant of time t= 0.012, 0.031 &0.0059. The variation of maximum temperature at different flow rate *Pe* = 1888 is shown in Figure 7.6.

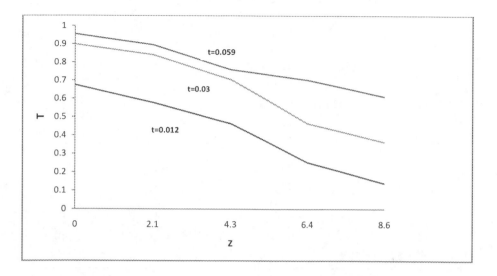

Figure 7.6: Variation of maximum temperature at different locations in steel water bed d_p =6.5 mm, *Pe= 1888,* ω= *0.0349 rad/s &* time t= 0.012, 0.031 &0.059

It is observed from the above graphs that the value of temperature at Z=0 (hot domain) is highest and decreases with stream. The value of peak temperature is low at time t= 0.012 and increases at time t= 0.059. The value of maximum temperature at high *Pe* is high as compared to high *Pe* due to the fluid exchanges more energy with solid material during in the same time period and the temperature increase is more. The temperature of thermocouple at exit end Z=8.6 is lower in case of low *Pe,* due to maximum amount of energy is exchanged in previous locations.

The value of minimum temperature varies with the locations. As the cold water is flowing in the opposite direction, the lowest value should be at cold domain. The valley temperature is at three time t= 0.024, 0.037 & 0.053. The variation of valley temperature at *Pe* = 1888 is shown in Figure 7.7.

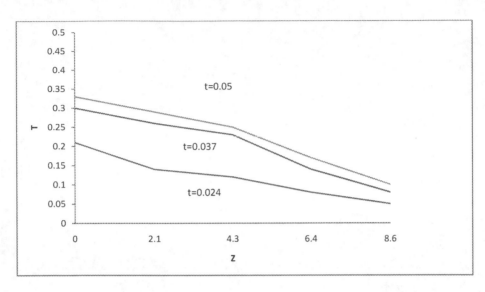

Figure 7.7: Variation of minimum temperature at different locations steel water bed d_p =6.5 mm, *Pe= 1888,* ω= *0.0349 rad/s &* time t= 0.012, 0.031 &0.059

Figure 7.7 shows that minimum temperature is at location Z= 8.6 as the cold water enters at cold domain. The value of temperature increases as approaches hot domain Z = 0 to value of 0.33 at time t = 0.059 because the cold water takes the energy from solid material. The value of minimum temperature increases with time as shown at t= 0.053. It is concluded that the value of temperature increases from cold domain to hot domain and increases with time.

In hot phase it is shown that the temperature rise in steel bed II is slow as compared to steel water bed I and glass water bed. It is observed that temperature rises smoothly in hot phase and reaches maximum value, where as glass water bed the rise of temperature is sharp and then remains at the peak temperature for short period. The comparison of rise of temperature in hot phase at Z=0 is stall and glass bed is shown in Figure 7.8.

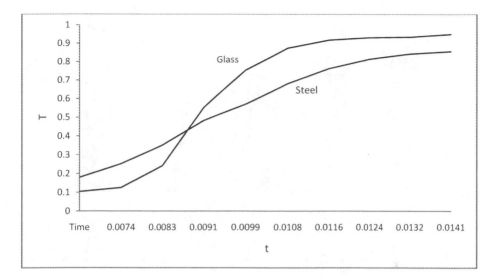

Figure 7.8: Comparison of temperature rise in glass and steel bed Z=0, ω= *0.0349 rad/s* and *Pe =1542*

It is observed from the comparison graph that the rise of temperature in steel water bed II is very slow as compared to the glass water bed. It shows that heat observed in steel water bed II is large as compared to glass water bed. As both the experiments are carried out on the same flow rate and non dimensional value is calculated. It concludes that more amount of heat is absorbed in steel water bed II due to the higher conductivity of steel and higher heat capacity ratio.

7.3 FRONT AMPLITUDE AND PHASE LAG

The flow of fluid in the steel water bed II is oscillatory in which the hot and cold flows alternately at opposite ends. The flow of hot and cold fluid in the bed creates a maximum and minimum temperature. The difference of the maximum and the minimum temperature is called the front amplitude. The front amplitude is analyzed at three Pe = 1368, 1542 & 1888. The front amplitude is calculated at different time t_1= 0.014, t_2= 0.029 & t_3= 0.044 and at all locations as shown in bar chart in Figure 7.9. The Figure 7.10 & 7.11 shows the variation of amplitude with the location at Pe = 1368 & 1888.

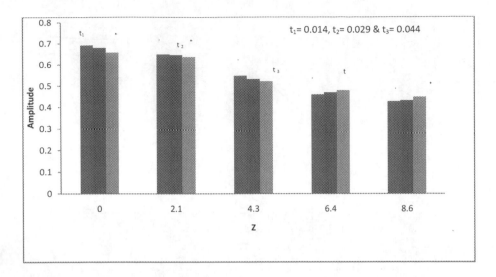

Figure 7.9: Variation of amplitude with locations in steel water bed d_p =6.5 mm at different time t_1= 0.014, t_2= 0.029 & t_3= 0.044 at *Pe= 1888 & ω= 0.0349 rad/s*

The bar chart in Figure 7.9 shows that amplitude is highest at time t_1= 0.014 at Z=0 and decreases with of time. Amplitude decreases with the locations but at locations Z= 6.4 & 8.6 the amplitude found increasing with time. At location Z= 2.1 the value of amplitude approximately uniform. The amplitude fluctuates in unsteady state and value approaches to each other at all the locations after four cycles. As compared to glass water bed the value of amplitude is low due to high thermal conductivity. Also the amplitude is less as compared to steel water bed I due to the increase of thermal capacity of bed with the large size of the porous material. It is concluded that amplitude decreases with the location and approaches to uniform value after four cycles when steady state is reached.

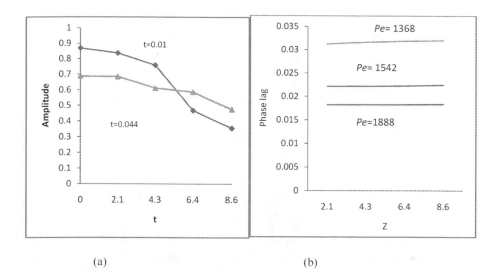

(a)　　　　　　　　　　　　　　(b)

Figure 7.10: Variation of (a) amplitude with locations at
Pe= 1888 (b) phase lag at different locations at
Pe= 1368, 1542 & 1888 in steel water bed *d*ₚ =6.5 mm & ω= 0.0349 rad/s

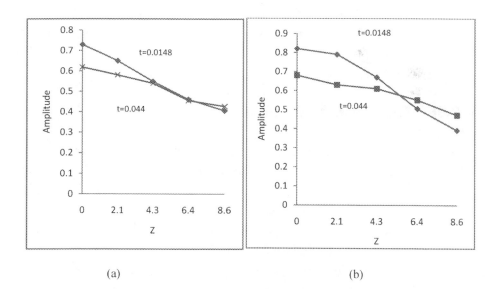

(a)　　　　　　　　　　　　　　(b)

Figure 7.11: Variation of amplitude with locations in steel water bed
*d*ₚ =6.5 mm at (a) *Pe =1368* (b) *Pe =1542 & ω= 0.0349 rad/s*

The Figure 7.10 (a) shows that the value of amplitude at higher flow rate Pe = 1888 is high. The value at Z= 0 The value of amplitude is 0.87 at hot domain Z= 0 and decreases in the successive cycles. Similar trends are observed for Z= 2.1 & Z= 4.3 but amplitude decreases at low rate. At Z= 8.6 the value of 1st cycles is low and increasing with the successive cycles. It is observed that at Pe =1888 the value of amplitude is approaching to each other after four cycles. The value of Z= 0 location decreases and the value of Z= 8.6 location increases from value of 0.4 to 0.5. The similar trends are obtained at Pe= 1542 but its value is less than at Pe = 1888. AT Pe = 1368 the value of amplitude is less at Z= 0 as 0.61 which is less as compared to value in steel water bed at Z= 0. It is observed that the value of amplitude in first two thermocouples decreases and in last three thermocouple increases. The rate of increase and decreases is very low. So it is concluded that the value of amplitude at high Pe is high because large amount of fluid is passing for same time period and low in steel water bed as compared to glass water value 0.93 at Pe = 2054 presented in Chapter 6. The value of steel water II is lower as 0.72 at Pe = 1368 as compared to 0.78 at Pe= 1287 of same location. The value of amplitude decreases with the increase of size of material. The value of temperature is maintained the same gap for two successive thermocouples. The phase lag is discussed at Pe= 1368, 1542 & 1888. The phase lag is almost similar to the phase lag in steel water bed I & glass water bed. The phase lag is constant at all locations and increases with increase in flow rate.

7.4 FRONT SPEED AND FRONT SPREAD

The thermal speed of fluid and the corresponding spread in the steel water bed is discussed in this section. As the front speed is the ratio of ΔZ and Δt, it is the change of 0.5 temperature at various locations. It is calculated for both hot and cold phase. The front speed is discussed at Pe = 1542 & 1888. The Figure 7.13 (a) shows the variation of front speed with the location. The front spread is rise of temperature from 0.25 to 0.75 at a location. The spread arises from spreading of fluid particle in both longitudinal and transverse direction. The spread increases with distance which results from spreading fluid particles in the transverse directions. Higher is the dispersion and heat less and higher is the spread. The front spread is an indicative of dispersion which decreases with increase in Pe. The dispersion increases the effective thermal conductivity of the fluid and solid phases (A lazmi & Vafai) which decrease the front spread. The front spread is analyzed at two flow rate *Pe* =1542 & 1888 and shown in Figure 7.13(b). The front speed and spread is calculated for hot and cold phase at *Pe*= 1888. The value for hot and cold phase is shown in bar chart in Figure 7.12.

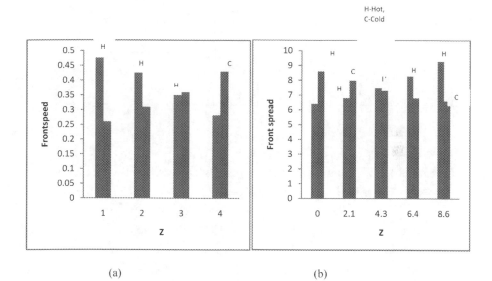

(a)   (b)

Figure 7.12: Variation(a) front speed (b) front spread with locations in steel water bed d_p =6.5 mm at *Pe =1888 & ω= 0.0349 rad/s*

Figure 7.12 (a) shows that front speed is highest for hot phase at location Z= 0 at a value of 0.47and decreases with downstream. The value decreases sharply with the locations. It is minimum at location Z= 8.6 at value of 0.38. The value of front speed is high at cold domain for the cold phase and decreases towards the hot domain as the cold water is entering at cold domain. It is observed that the value for hot and cold is almost equal at the end of the phase.

The front spread is minimum at location Z= 0 of value 0.63 and increases with the distance in the hot phase. Its value increases to 9.2 at location Z= 8.6. Similarly the value of spread is low in cold domain and increases with distance. The maximum value of front spread is higher in hot phase. The value for hot and cold phase at end phase is equal.

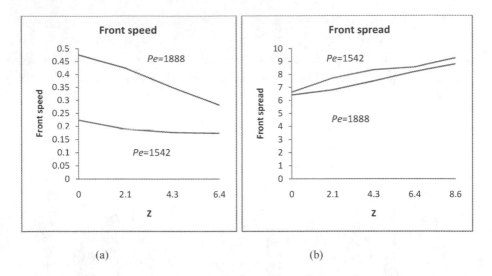

(a)   (b)

Figure 7.13: Variation of (a) front speed (b) front spread with locations in steel water bed d_p =6.5 mm, *Pe =1542& 1888* ω= *0.0349 rad/s*

The Figure 7.13 (a) shows that at *Pe* = 1542 the value of speed at location Z= 0 is 0.22 and reduces to 0.174 at location Z= 8.6. At flow rate *Pe* = 1888 the value of front speed at location Z= 0 is 0.47 and subsequently reduces to 0.28 at location Z= 8.6. It was concluded that front speed decreases with the locations and front spread increases with increase in flow rate. The value of front speed is less than the glass water bed of value 0.58 at *Pe* = 1542. The value of front speed was same for steel water bed and glass water bed I. The ratio of decreases of front speed at *Pe* = 1888 is very less. The thermal velocity of fluid at higher *Pe* is reducing at low rate.

It is observed from the graph that the front spread increases with the distance. The value of front spread at *Pe* = 1542 is increasing from 6.63 in the bed and at higher *Pe* =1888 the value rises from 6.41. The value of front spread is low at higher *Pe*. The value increases with the distance in both the cases. The spread and speed is analyzed after the cold phase and similar trends were observed. The fronts spread increases with increase in distance. The front spread is low at higher flow rate. So the experiment predicts the accurate result for speed and spread.

7.5 THERMAL NON EQUILIBRIUM

A significant temperature difference exists between solid and liquid phase during transit state of hot and cold phase. As the thermal conductivity of steel is higher and greater than water, thermal non equilibrium arises due to difference of these thermal properties. The thermal non equilibrium is obtained by 2 equation model which provide differentiable temperature profile for solid and liquid phases. In the previous chapter the thermal non equilibrium of steel water bed I and glass water bed was discussed. In the steel water bed II the spherical steel balls of 6.5 mm diameter are used as solid material. The effective surface area of solid material is 526.15 m^2/m^3 which is large for inter phase heat transfer between fluid and solid. In this experimentation the tube length 660 mm is used for analysis. The experiments are carried out at three different flow rate and different inlet hot water temperature. The temperature differences at all the locations were recorded. A solid material thermocouple was inserted in parallel to $Z = 6.4$ location. The flow of fluid is oscillatory in hot and cold fluid flows alternately and temperature fluctuates between maximum and minimum value. In the hot phase thermal non equilibrium is considered as positive in which fluid temperature is higher than solid material. The cold phase is considered as negative in which solid temperature is higher than fluid temperature. The difference of solid and liquid temperature recorded is shown in Table 7.2 ($Pe = 1368$).

Table 7.1: Interphase thermal non equlibrium in steel water bed d_p =6.5 mm size at Pe=1368

Cycle	1	2	3	4
Maximum thermal non equilibrium at Pe= 1368	0.047	0.035	0.032	0.028
Minimum thermal non equilibrium at Pe = 1368	-0.026	-0.31	-0.029	-0.028

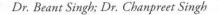

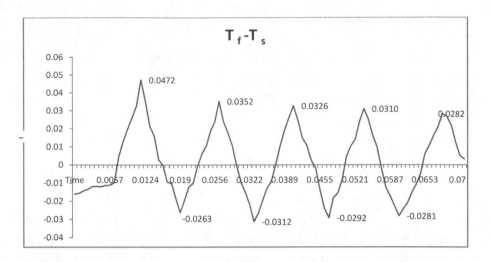

Figure 7.14: Variation of thermal equilibrium in steel water bed, d_p =6.5 mm size at *Pe= 1368, Z = 6.4 &* ω*= 0.0349 rad/s*

The value of thermal equilibrium is positive in hot flow and negative for cold flow. Maximum value for thermal equilibrium is higest in first cycle and decrease with distance. The minmum value is low in first cycle and increases in successive cycles. The amount of heat energy stored in first cycle is large and energy retrived is low. The amount of energy stored and retrival in the successive cycles closes to each other. Value of thermal equilibrium for large porous size is large as compared to steel water bed I. The value of thermal equilibrium for low conductive material is low. It concludes that the thermal equilirium increases with increase in size and increases with incre ase in conductivity.

7.6 THERMAL STORAGE OF ENERGY

The heat transfer by fluid moving particles through a porous matrix is phenomenon of great interest from the theory and application point of view. Heat transfer in case of fluid saturated porous has been studied with relation to different applications like dynamics of springs, tonsorial heat flow through aquifer, heat exchange between soil and atmosphere. In this section the heat storage in steel water bed II is discussed. The heat stored or retrieval is obtained by using fixed porous solid spherical steel beads through which hot or cold fluid oscillates. The heat exchange in steel water bed I was discussed in previous chapter in which steel beads of 4.55 mm diameter was used. In this experimentation steel beads of diameter 6.5 mm is used with effective surface area 526.15 m^2/m^3. Value of thermal non equilibrium between solid and fluid affects amount of heat storage. The hot and cold fluid flows alternately in porous bed at constant head. Hot phase is considered as positive phase in fluid temperature is higher than solid material. During the cold phase solid temperature is higher and considered as negative phase. Heat energy is stored in porous media in positive phase (hot phase) and retrieved in negative phase (cold phase). The stored energy over a time period can be calculated by the difference of energy levels between two time limits. Amount of energy stored is calculated by the energy equations explained in the previous chapter. In this experimentation the heat energy stored and retrieved is calculated at two Re number and presented graphically. As the effective surface area of the bed is different from the steel water bed I, energy stored by the bed will also be distinct. The variation of energy stored and retrieved at Pe = 1368 and 1888 is shown in Figure 7.15 &7.16.

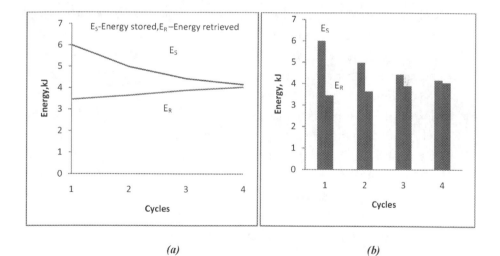

(a)   (b)

Figure 7.15: Energy stored and retrieved in cycles in steel water bed d_p = 6.5 mm size at *Pe= 1888 &* ω= *0.0349 rad/s.* (a) Line Graph (b) Bar chart

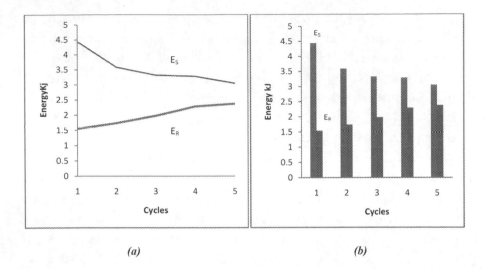

Figure 7.16: Energy Stored and Retrieved in cycles in steel water bed
d_p = 6.5 mm size at *Pe =1368 & ω= 0.0349 rad/s.*
(a) Line Graph (b) Bar chart

It is observed that energy stored at *Pe* =1368 is 4.18 kJ and retrieved is 1.93 kJ in the first cycle. Amount of energy stored decreases with successive cycles and energy retrieved increases. The value of energy stored and retrieved approaches to each other after five cycles and effectiveness approaches to 0.1 value. At *Pe*= 1888 energy stored is higher 6.00 kJ in first cycle and energy retrieved 3.45 kJ. The similar trends are observed for the successive cycles. The amount of energy exchange for large size of porous material is higher. At higher flow rate the amount of energy exchanged is increase as shown at *Pe* =1888. It is concluded that with the increase in particle size, the amount of energy stored and retrieved is increased. As the thermal conductivity of steel is higher than glass, the energy exchange in steel water bed is large. With the increase in conductivity the amount of energy exchanged is increased.

7.7 COMPARISON OF FREQUENCY RESPONSE

The frequency response for steel water bed I d_p = 4.55 mm, glass water bed d_p = 6.5 mm and steel water bed II d_p = 6.5 *mm* is discussed. The temperature profiles for three beds at location Z= 4.3 is shown in Figure 7.17. The temperature profile is shown for one cycle is considered in the sreday state.

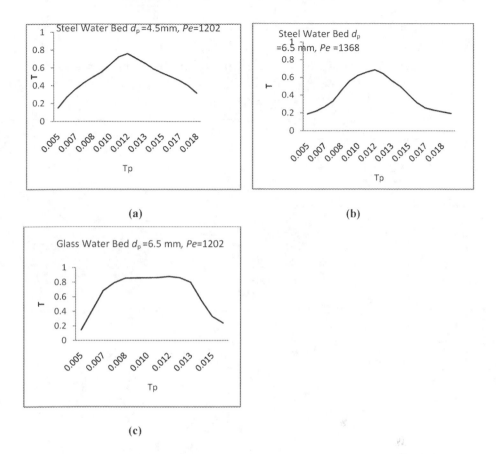

Figure: 7.17: Comparison of frequency response at Z=4.3 (a) Steel Water Bed d_p = 4.5mm, *Pe* = 1202, (b) Steel Water Bed d_p = 6.5 mm, *Pe* = 1368, (c) Glass Water Bed d_p =6.5 mm, *Pe* = 1202 at ω = 0.034 *rad/s*.

It is observed that there is sharp rise and fall of temperature in glass water bed and temperature retains a peak for some period of time. The glass material takes less time to reach peak value due to low thermal conductivity. In steel water bed I the temperature rise to peak value at slow rate than glass water bed. The same trend is observed in steel water bed II but the shape of graph is different. The temperature rise in steel water bed II is having low slope. It is concluded that in steady state temperature rises sharply in glass water bed due to low thermal conductivity. The rise of temperature is slow for large particle size.

The amplitude for three beds were compared at the flow rate for steel water bed I at *Pe* = 1287, steel water bed II at *Pe* = 1888 and glass water bed at *Pe* =1542. The similar trends were obtained in all three beds. The comparison is shown in following Figure 7.18.

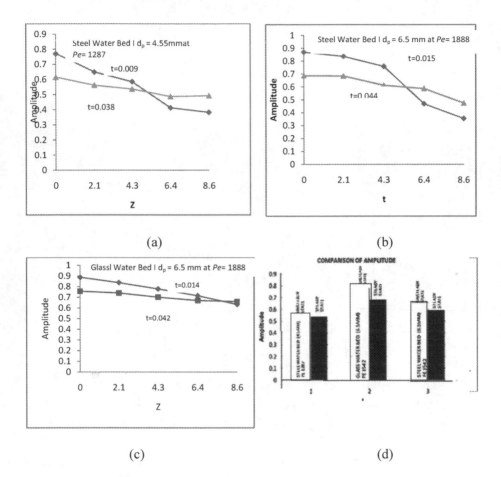

(a)

(b)

(c)

(d)

Figure 7.18: Comparison of amplitude at ω = 0.34 rad/s;
(a) Steel Water Bed I at *Pe=1287* (b) Steel Water Bed at *Pe = 1888*
(c) Glass Water Bed at *Pe = 1542* (d) Comparison
of average amplitude in three beds.

It is concluded that front amplitude is higher for glass material due to sharp rise of temperature to maximum value. Amplitude near the hot domain is high and decreases with passage of time. The value of amplitude is higher for large particle size due to smaller effective area.

The front speed is thermal speed of fluid and it is different from fluid speed. The front speed is calculated at different flow rate for three beds. The front speed compared for steel water bed I at *Pe*= 1202, for glass water bed at *Pe*= 1888 and steel water bed II at *Pe*= 1542 and shown graphically in Figure 7.19.

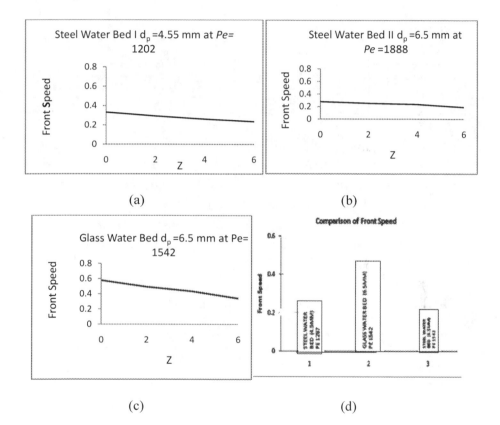

(a)

(b)

(c)

(d)

Figure 7.19: Comparison of front speed at $\omega = 0.034$ *rad/s*;
(a) Steel Water Bed at *Pe* = 1202 (b) Steel Water Bed at *Pe* = 1888
(c) Glass Water Bed at *Pe* = 1542 (d) Comparison of average front speed.

Table 7.2: Comparison of Front Speed in
different Porous Beds at ω=0.034 rad/s

Particle Size and Material	Pe	Front speed	
		Maximum	Minimum
4.55mm Steel	1202	0.33	0.23
	1287	0.30	0.19
6.5mm Glass	2054	0.82	0.4
	1542	0.57	0.33
6.5mm Steel	1888	0.27	0.18
	1542	0.22	0.17

The similar trends are obtained for three beds. The value of front speed decreases with increase in particle size as the large amount of heat is absorbed by large particle. Its value is higher for glass material due to low thermal conductivity as the heat flows at fast rate.

The front spread is the distribution of heat in longitudinal and transverse directions. In this heat moves in both directions. The Front spread is compared for three beds and shown in Figure 7.20.

Table No: 7.3 Comparison of Front Spread in different Porous beds

Particle Size and Bed	Pe	Front Spread	
		Maximum	Minimum
4.55 mm Steel	1287	7.93	5.14
	1202	6.6	4.4
6.5 mm Glass	2054	8.54	3.08
	1542	7.65	2.55
6.5 mm Steel	1888	11.77	6.41
	1542	10.7	6.63

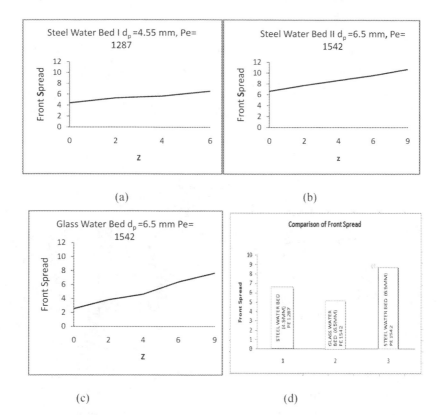

Figure 7.20: Comparison of front spread at ω=*0.0345 rad/s*;
(a) Steel Water Bed at *Pe = 1202 (b)* Steel Water Bed at *Pe = 1888*
(c) Glass Water Bed at *Pe = 1542 (d)* Comparison of average Front Spread.

It is concluded from above graphs that front spread increases with increase in particle size. Its value is lower for glass material of same size.

7.8 COMPARISON OF ENERGY STORAGE

Heat energy stored and retrieved for the different material and size is discussed in previous articles at different flow rate. Amount of energy is calculated for each cycle. The energy exchanged depends upon thermal properties of solid and fluid phases. The experiments are performed at frequency ω =0.034 rad/s and amount of energy is obtained by the energy equations at various flow rates. The amount of energy stored and retrieved with respect to cycles for three beds are shown in Figures 7.21.

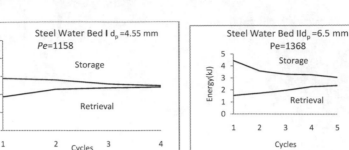

(a)   (b)

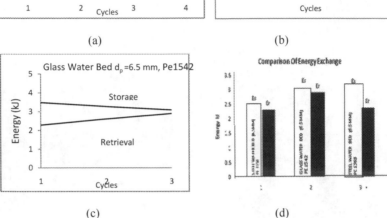

(c)   (d)

Figure 7.21: Comparison of energy exchange at ω=0.0345 *rad/s*;
(a) Steel Water Bed at *Pe*=1158 (b) Steel Water Bed at *Pe*=1368
(c) Glass Water Bed at *Pe*=1542 (d) Comparison of
energy stored and retrieved in three beds.

Table: 7.4 Comparison of Energy Storage in various Porous Beds

Particle Size and Bed	Pe	Energy Stored at Steady State(kJ)	Energy Retrieved at Steady state(kJ)
4.55 mm Steel	1158	2.47	2.39
	1287	2.86	2.73
6.5 mm Glass	1629	3.42	3.18
	1542	3.08	2.89
6.5 mm Steel	1888	3.86	2.97
	1368	3.04	2.37

It is observed that the difference of energy stored and retrieved is large during the initial (unsteady state) stage and reduces in successive cycles when steady state is reached. The effectiveness approaches to 0.1 in the steady state. In steel water bed I (4.55 mm size) the amount of energy stored is less and energy stored & retrieved approaches each other due to steady state. Amount of energy stored by large particles high as compared to small size particles. Also the amount of energy stored by steel particles is low as compared to glass material of same size.

Thermal equilibrium plays an important role for heat exchange. Value of thermal non equilibrium is high for large particle size as compared in the steel beds. Its value is low for glass material for same material size.

7.9 HEAT LOSS IN POROUS BED

The experimental analysis for the thermal response is carried for solid material size of steel ball 4.55 mm, glass ball 6.5 mm and steel ball 6.5 mm. It is observed from the number of experiments in three porous beds that temperature of the hot water tank is higher than the temperature of thermocouple inserted at hot domain. As the flow of fluid in bed is turbulant and non Darcian, small amount of energy is lost. From the heat energy calculations, it is observed that heat energy stored in each cycle is higher than the energy retrieved. The difference of heat stored and retrieved is considered as heat loss. The amount of heat loss in three beds at various flow rate is shown in folloing tables.

Table 7.5: Thermal storage & retreval calculations
in steel water bed, d_p =4.55mm *at Pe*=1158

cycles	Energy Storage (kJ)	Energy Retrieval (kJ)	Heat Loss (kJ)
1	2.88	1.86	1.02
2	2.79	2.27	0.52
3	2.57	2.35	0.22
4	2.47	2.39	0.09

Table 7.6: Thermal storage & retreval calculations in
steel water bed (4.55mm Size) at *Pe*= 1202

cycles	Energy Storage (kJ)	Energy Retrieval (kJ)	Heat Loss (kJ)
1	2.207	1.900	0.307
2	1.856	1.740	0.126
3	1.738	1.621	0.117
4	1.698	1.594	0.104

Table 7.7: Thermal storage & retreval calculations in
glass water bed (6.5mm Size) at *Pe*= 1629

cycles	Energy Storage (kJ)	Energy Retrieval (kJ)	Heat Loss (kJ)
1	3.733	2.563	1.170
2	3.591	2.567	1.024
3	3.391	2.618	0.773
4	3.260	2.859	0.401
5	3.176	3.062	0.114

Table 7.8 Thermal storage & retreval calculations in
steel water bed (6.5mm Size) at Pe =1368

cycles	Energy Storage (kJ)	Energy Retrieval (kJ)	Heat Loss (KJ)
1	4.188	1.937	2.251
2	3.805	2.101	1.704
3	3.310	2.408	0.902
4	3.247	2.690	0.557
5	3.080	2.968	0.112

It is observad that the energy lost in steel water bed I is less and reducing in successive cycles. The steel water bed II (6.5 mm Size) has large specific area and consumes large amount of heat during hot flow and large amount of heat is retrived. It is concluded that with the increase in size of particle, the amount of heat lost is increased. In glass water bed the amount of heat loss is large, as the thermal conductivity of material is low and unable to store large amount of energy. In steel water bed, in steel balls of 6.5 mm size is used, the energy loss is large due to low frequency and porous bed unable to retrieve the whole energy in initial cycles but amount of retrieved energy increases in successive cycles and energy lost is decreased. It is included that in small size porous bed the heat energy loss is less as compared to the large size porous bed, also with the increase of flow rate, energy loss is increased.

7.10 CLOSURE

The frequency response of steel water bed II was discussed in this chapter. The solid material used for experimentation was spherical steel balls of 6.5 mm diameter. The thermal conductivity of steel is higher than glass material and effective surface area is less. The rise and fall of temperature in hot and cold phase were found very gentle. The maximum temperature rise in hot phase is low as compared to glass water bed and steel water bed I for the same time period. The experiment was performed at three flow rate Pe = 1368, 1542 and 1888. Temperatures profiles obtained with respect to time were in the sine wave form but different from the glass water bed. Rise of temperature is very low at cold domain thermocouple. The rise of temperature increases with the increase in flow rate. The front amplitude was found to be decreasing with distance and value is low as compared to glass water bed. The decrease rate amplitude with distance is very low. The temperature gap between location Z= 0 and Z= 6.4 were found to increasing. The front speed at Pe= 1888 and 1542 is observed as decreasing with locations. The value for front speed is higher for steel water bed II. The thermal equilibrium obtained was in the cyclic wave form. The amplitude was higher than glass water bed. The energy stored and retrieved calculated from two flow rate. The difference between amounts of energy stored and retrieved were large during initial stage and approaches to each other after few cycles. The amount of energy stored is large as compared glass water bed and steel water bed I. The thermal parameters like temperature profile, front amplitude. Front speed, front spread are compared in three beds at frequency value of 0.034. The variations of these thermal parameters are analyzed.

CHAPTER 8

CONCLUSION AND SCOPE
OF FUTURE WORK

8.1 INTRODUCTION

The present work focused on to study the thermal non equilibrium for heating-cooling in porous media. Experimental study of porous media with reference to frequency response and energy storage is carried out during oscillating flow at different flow rate. A small scale lab experimental set up with required accuracy and repeatability was developed. The number of experiments was performed to study the frequency response at different boundary conditions in fully saturated flow. The three different beds of different particle size of glass and steel material were used for observation. The digital observations are obtained from experimental set up for result and calculations. The thermal parameters and energy stored/retrieval is presented graphically.

8.2 SUMMARY

The main aim of this research work to study the thermal non equilibrium for heating and cooling in oscillating flow thermal response and energy storage characteristics in porous media. The detail of present work is as follow

1. To carry out the literature survey for oscillating flow and interface heat transfer in porous media to study the thermal response and energy exchange. The focused is made for different material and different particle size.
2. A small scale lab experiment set up is fabricated as per the design parameters. The accuracy and repeatability of mechanical parts and

experiments is assured with calibration. The experiment provided digital information for further calculation.

3. The results of experiments are obtained by considering momentum and energy equation for non Darcian and saturated flow.

4. Oscillating flow is observed in which the hot fluid enters from hot domain and rises the temperature to peak value and cold fluid enters at opposite end reduces the temperature to lower value. The frequency response of bed is studied for front amplitude; front speed and front spread parameters.

5. Amount of energy stored and retrieved is obtained through a computerized program of energy equation. The comparison of energy stored and retrieved is shown in graphical form. The comparison of frequency response and energy storage in made by considering the three porous bed.

8.3 CONCLUSION

The frequency response and energy storage for different materials and particle size is studied for three different porous beds in oscillating flow at various flow rate. The following conclusions are made:

1. In steel water bed I (4.55 mm size) the value of front amplitude at location Z=0 near hot domain is higher and decreases with downstream. The value of front spread is higher at high Peclet number and value increases with distance. The phase lag is observed as uniform in all the cycles. The front speed is high at higher Peclet number and its value decreases with distance. Value of thermal non equilibrium fluctuates between positive and negative value. Its value is higher for hot phase. Amount of heat energy stored is large than heat energy retrieved in initial cycles but coming closer in successive cycles. Amount of heat energy is large at high Peclet number.

2. In glass water bed (6.5mm size) temperature rises sharply and value of amplitude is high. The value of front spread increases with distance and its value is high at higher Peclet number. The value of front speed decreases with distance. Thermal non equilibrium value fluctuates between positive and negative value. Its value is higher in hot phase.

Amount of heat energy stored is large than energy retrieved in initial cycles. The value of heat energy exchanged is high at high Peclet number.

3. In steel water bed II (6.5 mm Size) the temperature rises smoothly. Value of front amplitude is high at Z= 0 near the hot domain and its value at high flow rate is higher. The value of front speed is high at high Peclet number and decreases with distance. Front spread increases with the distance. Thermal non equilibrium value fluctuates between positive and negative value and its value is higher for hot phase. Amount of heat energy stored is large than energy retrieved in initial stage and coming closer in successive cycles. Amount of energy exchanged is less at higher flow rate.

4. On comparison it is concluded that front amplitude is higher for glass material. The value of front speed decreases with increase in particle size. Its value is higher for glass material. Front spread increases with increase in particle size. Its value is lower for glass material. Value of thermal non equilibrium is high for large particle size but its value is low for glass material. Amount of heat energy increases with increases in particle size. Its value is higher for steel material.

REFERENCES

[1] **A. Bahloul, P. Vasseur and L. Robillard** "Convection of a binary fluid saturating a shallow porous cavity subjected to cross heat fluxes". J.F Fluid Mechanics Vol. 574, pp 317-342 (2007).

[2] **AF Polyakov, V K start'ev, A.F. Tretyakov & YL Shekhter** "Heat transfer in Envelopes mode of porous Network Material" Thermal Engineering Vol 56 No. 3 pp 227-234

[3] **Arunn Narasimhanand B.V.K.Reddy** "Laminar forced convection in a heat generating bi-disperse porous medium channel" International Journal of Heat &Mass Transfer Vol. 54 issue 1-3 pp 636-644(2011)

[4] **B Straughan** "Global Non linear stability in porous convector with a thermal non-equilibrium model" Royal Society, Vol No. 462, pp 409-418(2006).

[5] **Bugbane, K. EL Generous and A.M. Kemp** "COMSOL 2D Simulation of heavy oil recovery by steam assisted gravity drainage". (International conference 2007)

[6] **Chanpreet Singh, R. G. Tathgir and K. Muralidhar** "Energy storage in fluid saturated porous media subjected to oscillatory flow" Heat and Mass Transfer, Vol. 45, pp427-441 (2009).

[7] **Chanpreet Singh** Convective Heat Transfer in Poous Media for Energy Storage: Unsteady Convective Heat Transfer in Liquid Saturated and Unsaturated Porous Media with reference to an Energy Storage System, Text Book VDM Verlag (2009), ISBN-10:3639198441.

[8] **D. A. Nield** "A Note on Local Thermal Non Equilibrium in Porous Media Near boundary and Interphases" Transp Porous Med 95, pp 581-584 (2012).

[9] **D. N. Riahi** "Study and oscillatory flow in a mushy layer" J. of Fluid mech. (1045, Mar 2004).

[10] **Donald A. Nield and Andrian Bejan:** Convection in Porous Media, A Text book, Springer

[11] **Francisco J. Valdes Parada and Jose Alvarez –Ramirez** "Frequency –dependent in porous media" Physical Review E84, 031201(2011) American Physical Society.

[12] **F. Pinson, O. Gregoire, M Quintard, M Prat, O. Simonin** "Modeling of turbulent heat transfer and thermal dispersion for flow in flat plate exchanger" International Journal of Heat &Mass Transfer Vol. 50, pp 1500-1515 (2007).

[13] **Gazy F.Al-Sumaily, Akira Nakayama, John Sheridan mark C. Thompson** "The effect of porous media particle size on forced convection from a circular cylinder without assuming local thermal equilibrium between phases" International Journal of Heat &Mass Transfer Vol. 55, pp 3366-3378 (2012)

[14] **Giovanni Cimatti** "Nearly explicit solution and uniqueness for the fluid flow and heat transfer in Porous media with temperate dependent viscosity" Journal of Mathematic Fluid Mech 19 Sep 2009.

[15] **Guillermo A Norsilio, Olivier Buzzi, Stephen Fityus, Tae Supyun, David W Smith** "Upscaling of Navier Stroke equations in porous media Theoratical, Numerical & Experimental approach Computers and Geotechnics" International Journal of Heat &Mass Transfer Vol. 36, pp-1200-1206 (2009).

[16] **H. Gull, Ecru Kava Apian** "Investigation of heat transfer and energy loss in oscillating circular pipes" Vol 34, issue 1pp93-102(2007).

[17] **J.C. Umavathi, AJ Camkha, A Mateen, A.AIMudhal** "Unsteady Oscillatory flow and Heat Transfer in a Horizontal Composite Porous Media Channel" Nonlinear Analysis, Vol: 14, No. 3, pp 397-415 (2009).

[18] **Jeo Young Kim, By My Hakay and Jae Min Hyun** "Heat Transfer from pulsating flow in channel filled with Porous Media" International Journal of Heat &Mass Transfer Vol. 37 (1994).

[19] **Jin Sheng heu, Jiin Yuh Jang, Yin Chou** "Heat and mass transfer for a liquid film International Journal of Heat &Mass Transfer, Vol. 49, pp 1937-1945 (2006).

[20] **Kambig Vafair & Kun Yang** "note on thermal non equilibrium in porous and heat flow bifurcation phenomenon is porous media Transp Porous Med Vol. 96, Issue 1, pp 169-172 (2013)

[21] **K.C.Leong, L W Jin** "Characteristics of oscillating flow through a channel filled with open-cell metal foam" International Journal of Heat &Mass Transfer Vol. 27, Issue1, pp144-153(2006).

[22] **K.C.Leong, L W Jin** "An experiment study of heat transfer in oscillating flow through channel filled with aluminum foam" International Journal of Heat &Mass Transfer Vol. 48, issue 2, pp243-253(2005)Elsevier.

[23] **K.C.Leong, L W Jin** "Effect of oscillatory on heat transfer in metal foam heat sink of various pore densities" International Journal of Heat &Mass Transfer Vol. 49 issue 3-4 pp 671-681(2005).

[24] **Khalil Khanafer** "Flow and heat transfer in biological tissues application of porous media theory" International Journal of Heat &Mass Transfer Vol. 22, pp 237-259 (2008).

[25] **Marcelo B. Salto and Marcelo J.S. de Lemos** "Laminar heat transfer in a porous channel simulated with a two energy equation model." International Communication in Heat and Mass TransferVol 36, issue 10,(2009).

[26] **Mehmet Turgey Pamuk, Mustafa ozdemir** "Heat transfer in Porous Media under oscillating flow" Experimental Thermal And Fluid Science Vol. 42 pp79-92 (2012).

[27] **M H Kayhani, A.O.Abbasi, M.Sadi** "Study of local thermal non equilibrium in porous media due to temperature sudden change and heat generation" Mechanics Vol. 17 No 1 (2011) KAUMAS University of Technology.

[28] **Michael X Maida** "IC Temperature sensor provides thermo couple Cold function Compensation" National Semiconductor. Application No. 225, April 1979 Texas Instrumentation.

[29] **M. Kaviany:** Principles of Heat Transfer in Porous Media, Text Book By Springer.

[30] **MM Hamza, BY Isah and H Usman** "Unsteady Heat Transfer to MHD Oscillatory Flow through Porous Medium under slip condition" IJCA Vol. 33 N0 4 (2011).

[31] **MM Rahman, T Sultana** "Radiative heat transfer flow of micropolor fluid with variable heat fluid in Porous Medium" Nonlinear Analysis Vol. 13 No. 71-87(2008).

[32] **Murlidhar and Sujuki** "Analysis of flow and heat transfer in porous media" International Journal of Heat &Mass Transfer Vol. 444 pp 3535-3563(2001).

[33] **Nakayama A., Kuwahara F. and S.ugiyama M.** "A two energy equation model for conduction and convection in porous media" International Journal of Heat &Mass Transfer Vol. 44 pp 4375-4379(2001).

[34] **N. Amanifard M. Borji, A.K. Haghi** "Heat transfer in Porous Media" Brazillian Journal of Chemical Engg. Vol. 24 No. 2 (2007).

[35] **Namgyum Jeong, Do Hyurychoi & Chiryhory** "Prediction of Darcy for Cwnieimer dray for micro porous structure of complex geometry using letter Bultzmarium method" Journal of Micromechanics and Microengineering Vol-16 (2006).

[36] **Pascale Bouvier, Pascal Stouffs and Jean-Pierre Bardon** "Experiment study of heat transfer in oscillating flow" I International Journal of Heat &Mass Transfer Vol. 48 issue 12 Jun (2005).

[37] **Poury Forooghi, Mahdi Abkor, Mazid Saffar Awal** "Steady and Unsteady Heat transfer in a channel partially filled With porous media under thermal Non-equilibrium Condition" International Journal of Heat &Mass Transfer Vol.86 issue pp 177-198 (2011).

[38] **PVSN Murthy and P Singh** "Heat and Mass transfer by natural convection in a Non Darcy Porous Medium" Acta Mechnica Vol No. 13 pp-243-254 (1999).

[39] **O.O.ALBI, O.I. POPOOLA and J.A. Adegoke** "Modification of fluid flow equation in saturated Porous Media" Global Journal of Pure and Applied Sci Vol 15, No. 3 pp-395-400(2009).

[40] **R.A. Mohamed** "Double-Diffusive Convection-Radiation Interaction on Unsteady MHD Flow over a Vertical Moving Porous Plate with Heat Generation and Sorest Effects" Applied Mathematical Science Vol 3, no 13 pp 629-651 (2009).

[41] **Roy Taw, Terry Simon, David Gideon, Mourner Brahman Weir Rung** "An Initiation Non-Equilibrium Porous-Media Model for CFD Simulation on sterling Regenerators" (4th International Energy Conf Diego, California 26-29Jun 2006).

[42] **San San Yee and Couch Kamiuto** "Theoratical Study of Heat Generation due to Viscous Dissipation in Adiabatic Packed- Bed Forced-Convection Flow" Vol. 12 issue 9(2000).

[43] **Seo Young Kim, Byung Ha Kang and Jae Min Hyun** "Heat transfer from pulsating flow in a channel filled with porous media" International Journal of Heat &Mass Transfer Vol. 37 issue 14 pp 2025-2033 (1994).

[44] **S. Frey, M. L. Martin-Costa and R. M. Saldanhadagama** "Petrov-Galerkin Approximation for Advective-Diffusive Heat Transfer in Saturated Porous Media" IJH&MT pp169-178 (2007)

[45] **Shadi Mahjoob, Kambiz Vafai** "A synthesis of fluid and thermal transport models for metal foam heat exchangers" International Journal of Heat &Mass Transfer Vol. 51 pp3701-3711(2008) Science Direct

[46] **S Mukhopadhyay G C Layak** "Radiation effect on forced convective flow and heat transfer over a Porous Plate in a Porous Media" Meccanica Vol 44 pp 587-597 (2009)Springer.

[47] **SS Das, A Satapathy, J K Das, J P Panda** "Mass transfer effect on MHD Flow and heat transfer post a vertical Porous Plate through a Porous Medium under oscillating suction and heat source" International Journal of Heat &Mass Transfer Vol. 52 pp 5962-5969(2009)

[48] **Sumrerng Jugjai and Chanon Chuenchit** "A study of energy conversion by a porous combustor-Heat Exchange with cycle flow Reversal Combustion" International Energy Journal Vol. 2 No. 2 (2000).

[49] **S. Y. Byun, S. T. Ro, J. Y.Shin, Y. S. Son and D.Y. Lee** "Transient thermal behavior of porous media under oscillating flow conditions" International Journal of Heat &Mass Transfer Vol. 49 issue 25-26 pp 5081-5085 (2006).

[50] **S.Z. Suja, B.S. Yibas** "Flow over rectangular porous block in a fixed width channel: influence of porosity and aspect ratio" IJof Fluid Dynamics Vol. 21 issue 7-8 pp 297-305 (2007).

[51] **M.G. Trefry, D.McLaughlin, G. Metcalfe, D. Lester, A. Ord, K. Regenauer-Lieb and B.E.Hobbs** "On oscillating flows in randomly heterogeneous porous media. Philoophical Transactions 368, pp-197-216(2010) Royal Society.

[52] **Unal Akdag, M. Aydin Komur, A. Feridun Ozguc** "Estimation of heat transfer in oscillating annular flow using artificial neural networks" Advance in Engineering Software Vol. 40 issue 9 pp864-870 (2009).

[53] **You-Minj Chen and Chung Young Sun** "Experimental Study on the heat and mass transfer of a combined absorber evaporator exchanger" Vol. 40 No. 4 pp-1971-1977 (1996).

[54] **Z.F. Sun and C.G. Carrington** "Oscillating Flow Modeling of a Stirling cycle cryocooler" A Cryogenic Engineering Conference Publications Vol. 41 pp 1543- 1550(1996).